Nankipoo Art

By
Lowell Tillman Jr.

Acrylic, Oils, And Pen/Ink

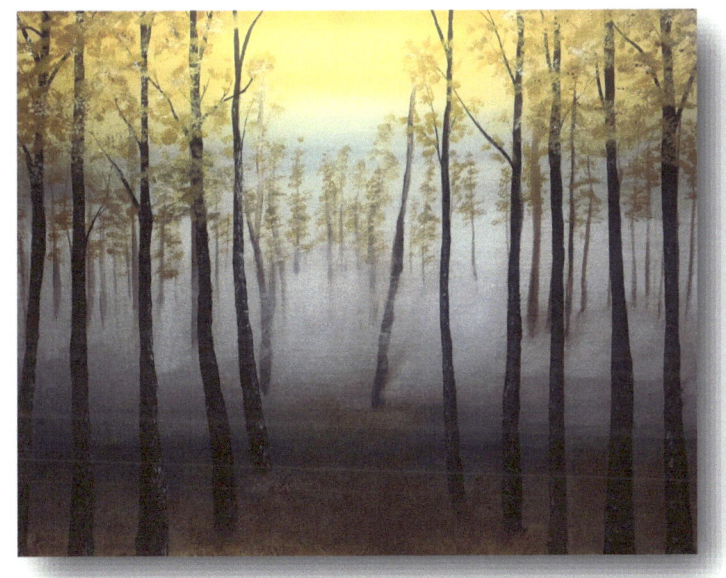

Copyright 2016

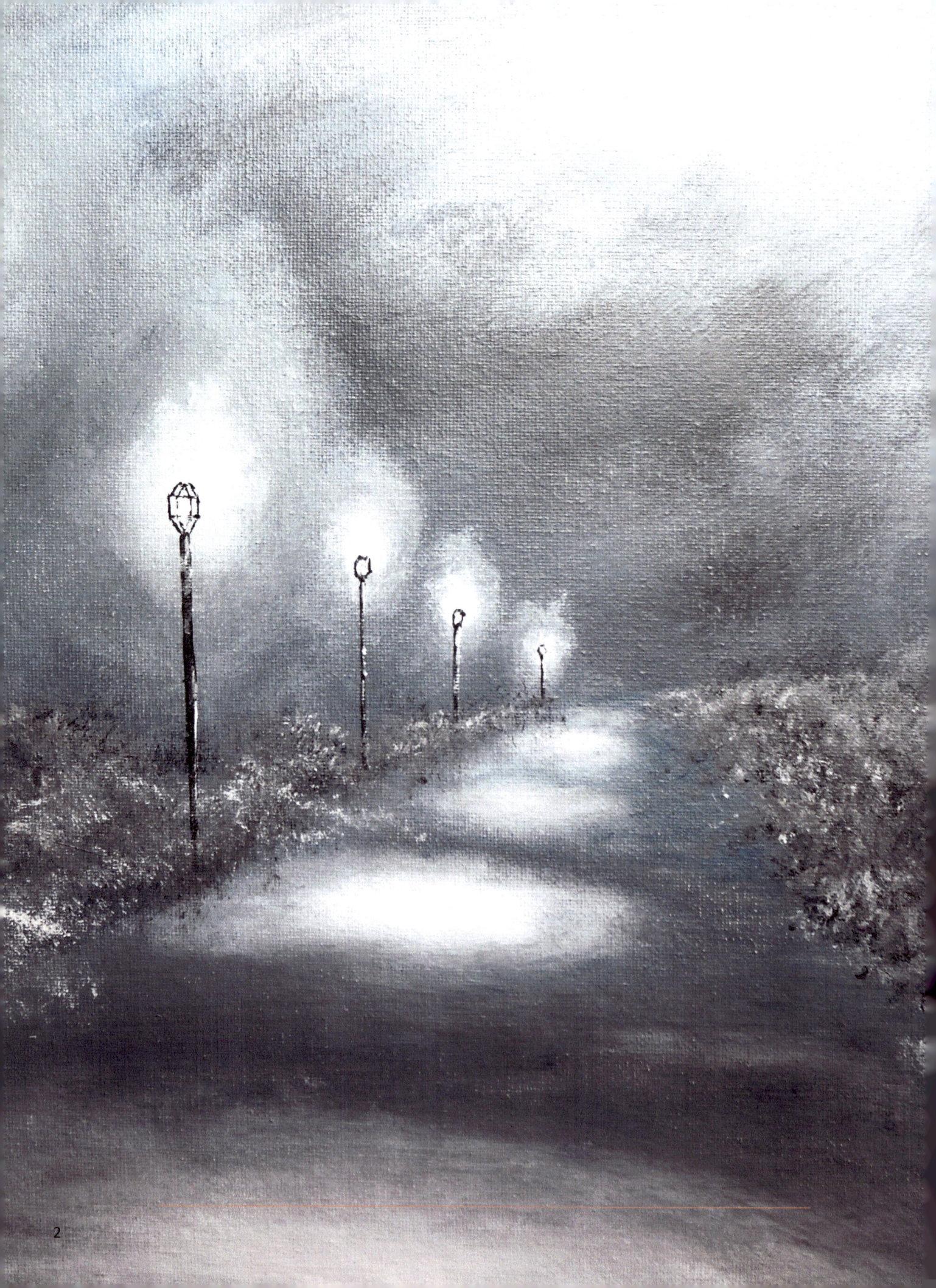

Nankipoo Art is a partial collection of ink sketches and paintings that I have done over the years. Some of the paintings date back to 1992 and some further. I hope others enjoy my work, as that's the primary reason why I paint. There are a few examples of oil paintings included in this collection. I experimented with that medium for several years, and I still enjoy using it from time to time. But, I find my patience is too short to allow for the proper drying time needed. Acrylics have their own unique ability of fast drying, and that can be an asset, as well as a complication. I find precision sharpies handy as they are very portable. You will find me many times in restaurants drawing with those. Several of the sketches included here were created during lunch stops at various restaurants (primarily McDonalds).

It is fascinating the number of people that come and talk to me while I'm sketching. That's why I call Art the *Universal Language*. Once, that did occur. A couple came up to me as I was sketching. They couldn't speak a word of English. And, I couldn't talk a note of whatever language they were speaking, but somehow, we did communicate. They smiled and pointed at my sketch. I handed them my sketchbook as they looked through the pages their smile broadened pointing at some of their favorites. They handed me back the sketchbook as they both bowed and left. I bow thanking you now, and I hope the universal language of art brings a smile to your day.

Dedication:

Of course, my mother Shelton. She was, and is still, an inspiration to me. My wife for being my muse. My daughter for being my best critique. My older sister for helping me with I was young. My father for his work ethic.

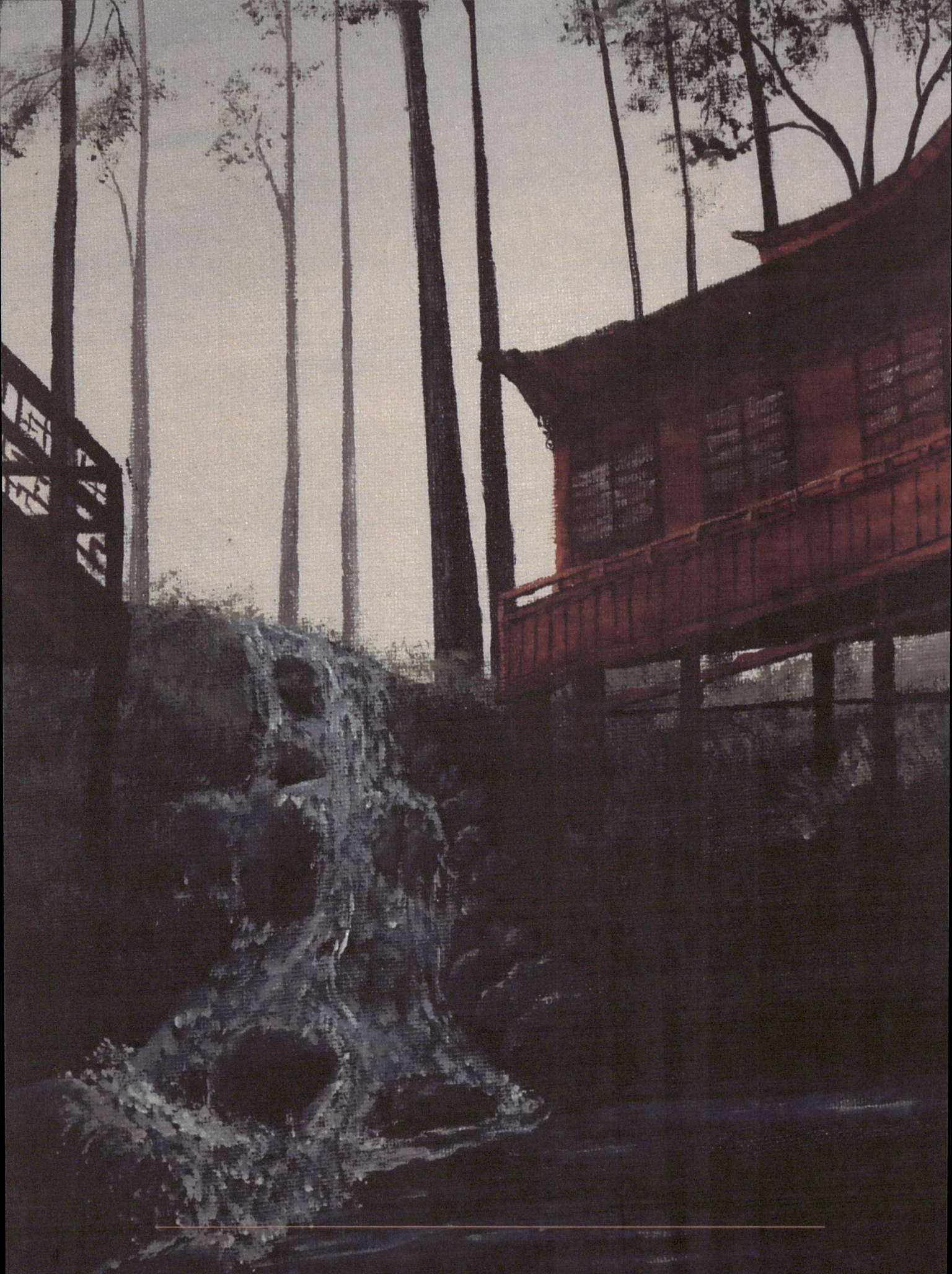

Nankipoo Tennessee, a small town in the north-western section of the state. It's a little community like so many around the area. Situated near the bluff above the delta basin flanking both sides of the Mississippi River the little area has gone through many changes during its history. In the nineteen hundreds, the Nankipoo school was a thriving two story education center piece. The girls high school basketball team won the state championship that year. Unlike most rural schools the Nankipoo school included all twelve grades. Also during this time no less than four general stores and two blacksmith shops dotted the area. It was only the invention and implementation of the railway system that spelled the doom of so many small towns, including Nankipoo. Many people moved toward the businesses and activities of the towns hosting these rails. One by one the stores closed and the blacksmith shops were converted into residences or torn down. Even after this exodus many people stayed attracted to the farm life style or perhaps just carrying on family traditions to keep the farms going. Through it all Nankipoo held on to the one thing that make this little town different than other little communities, its name, Nankipoo.

There have been many explanations, theories and urban legends to explain the origin of its name. When I was a child I believed the urban legend. It seemed logical, the legend was there had been an Indian tribe living here many years ago, and the name of their chief was Nankipoo. So, for years myself and many others beloved this quirky theory. The many arrow heads further supported the theory I would find on the hill behind my house. Many years later I decided to do some research of the true origin of the name. It seems that during the latter part of the seventeenth century a post master in the area called Key Corner and a fellow post master were discussing the need of a new post office box for the area of the crossroads of Cates, Edith Dry hill, and a little gravel road called Sammy Wright Rd today but at the time was known as something else, but its name is lost in time.

The post master had just returned from a trip to England and while there she had attended a play called Mikado. The production was a Japanese comic opera performed in two acts with music by Arthur Sullivan with libretto by W.S. Gilbert, a Savoy Theater production. The play opened in England March 1885. It went on to run for 672 performances. It was the second longest running musical theater of the time. The play featured two characters called Yum-yum and Nankipoo. The post master was quick to pick the quirky name fresh on her mind. Today, the web site Nankipoo.com and the Facebook page Nankipoo Historical Society is frequented by many visitors from Japan and others researching the play. The Facebook page Nankipoo Historical Society features a clip of the play as it was performed a few years ago, in Japan.

Featured in this book are paintings and drawing samples of my work. Some are representations of current landmarks in the little community, others are works simply inspired by the surroundings. A few paintings are Japanese inspired. I hope you enjoy these pages. Please visit http://nankipoot.wixsite.com/artsy for more information on Nankipoo Art.

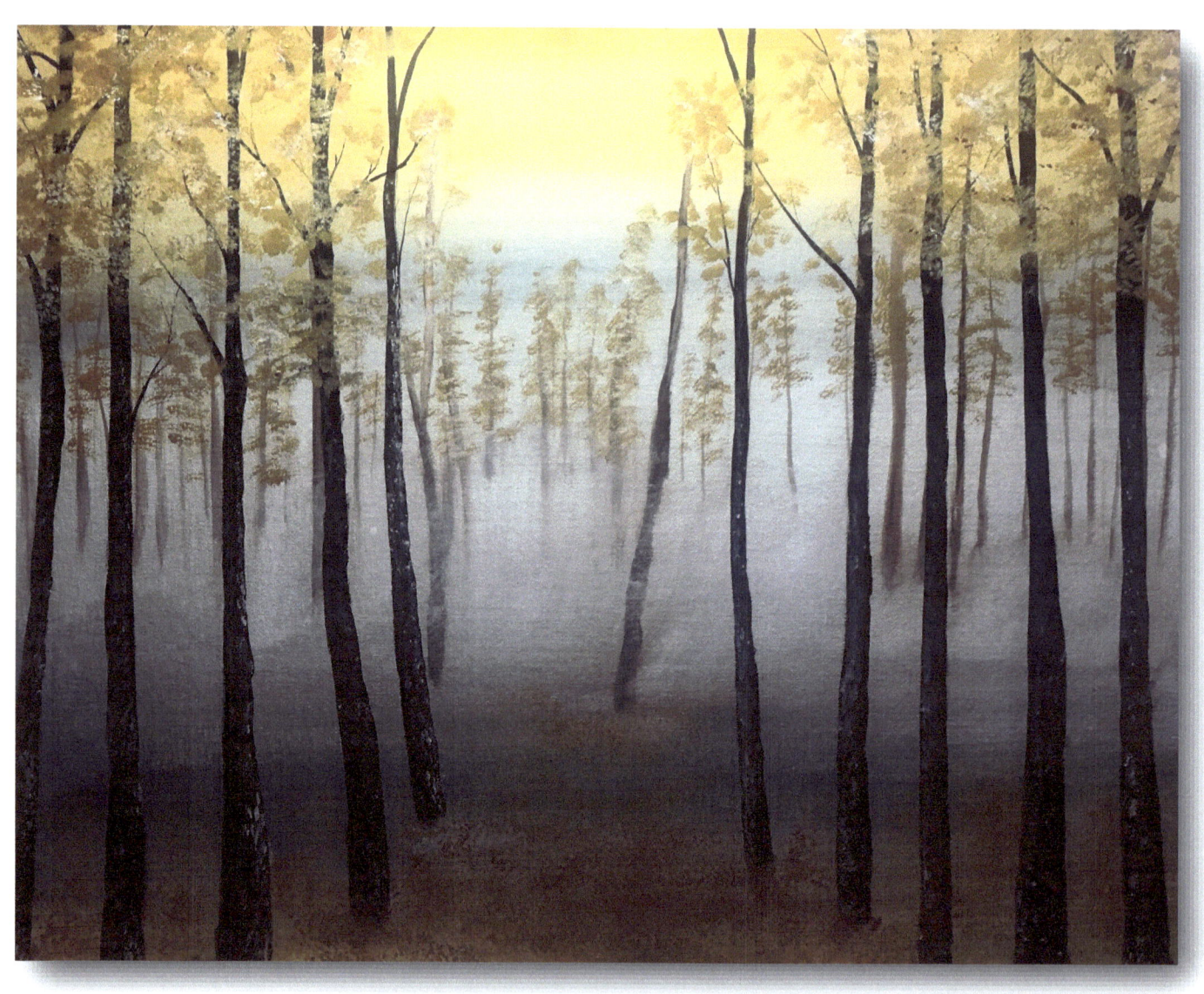

Misty

Acrylic 16x20 panel board

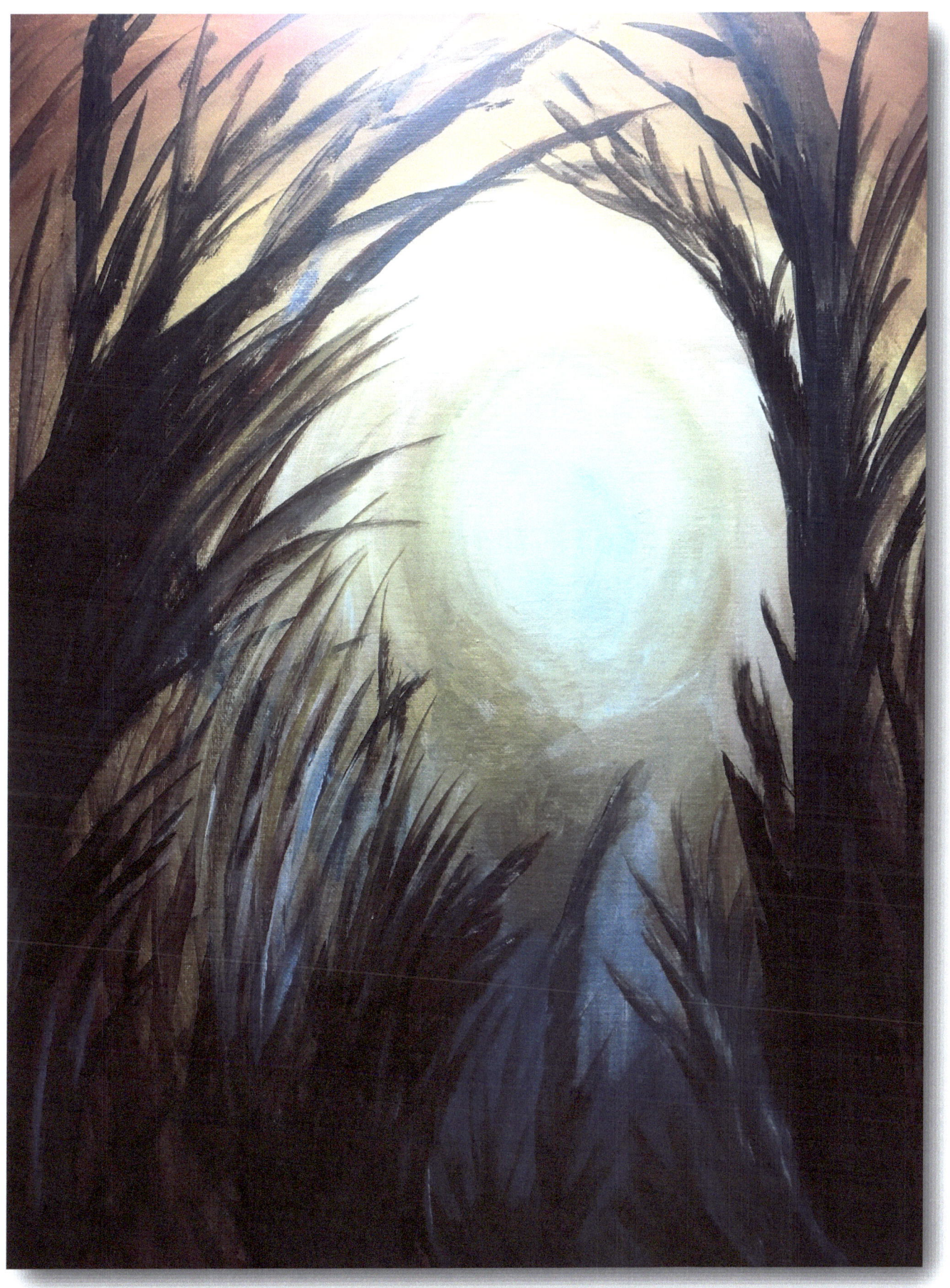

View from a Rabbit

Acrylic 16x20 panel board

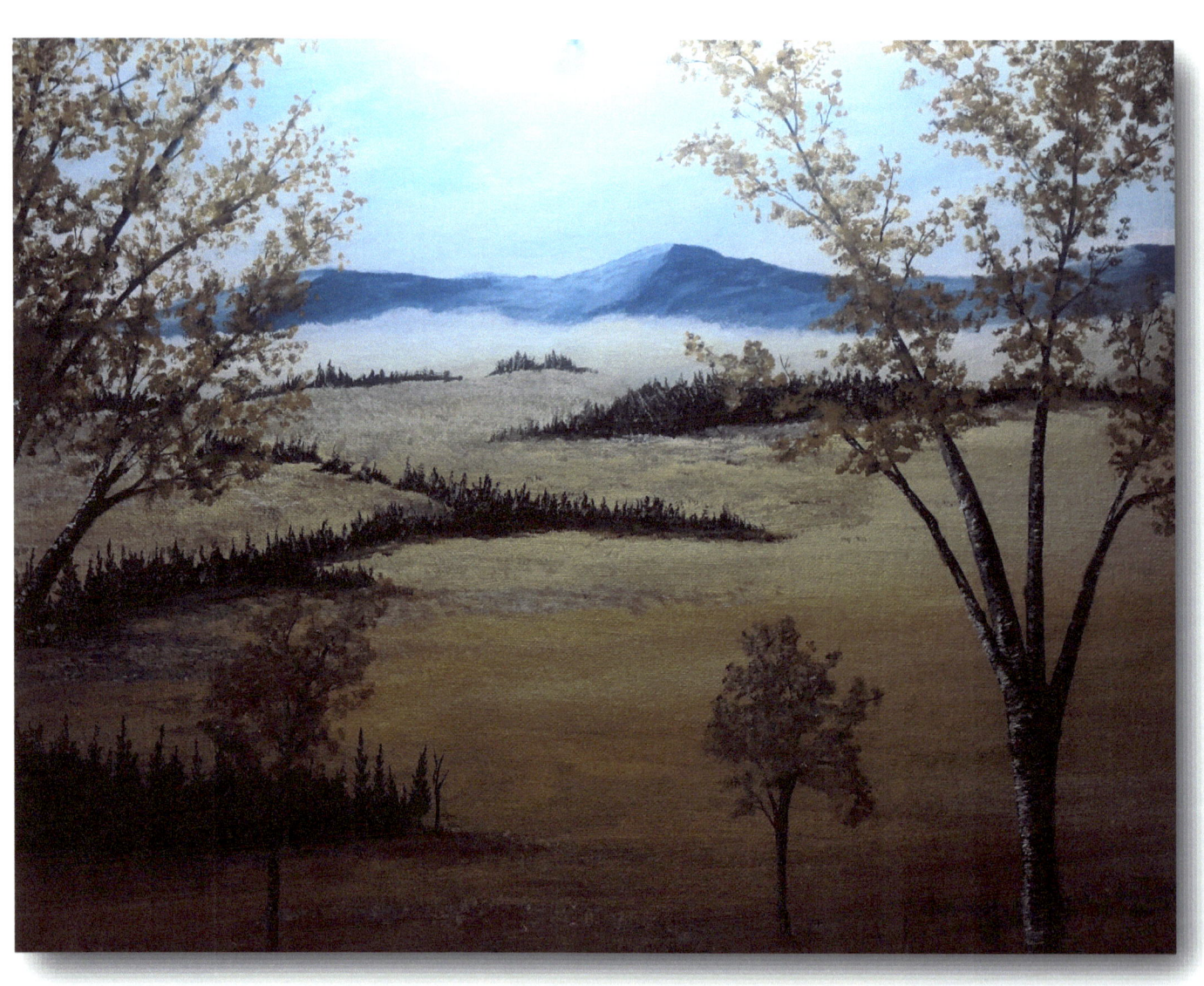

Hedgerows and Fields of Grain

Acrylic 16x20 panel board

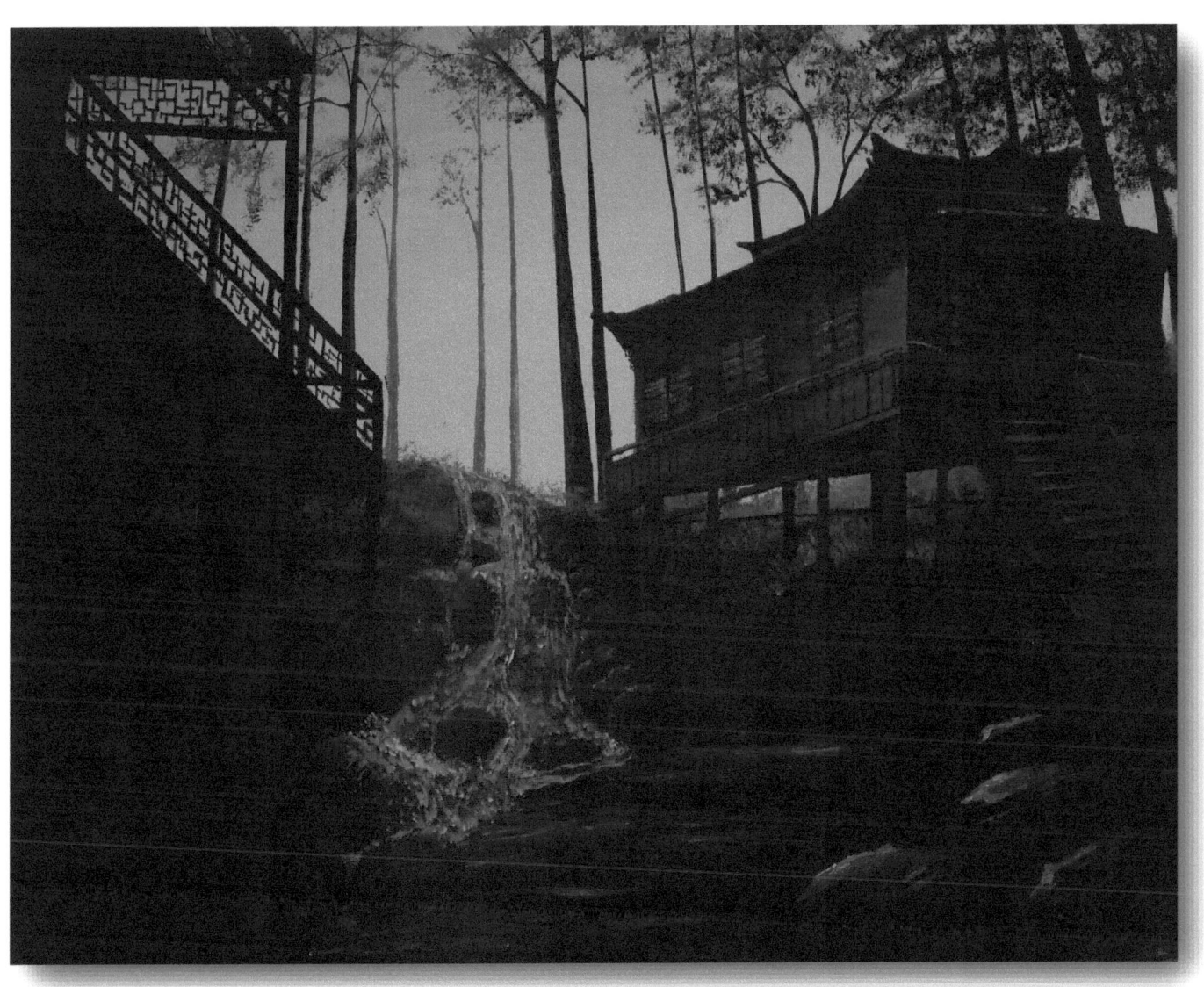

Temple Dreams

Acrylic 16x20 stretched canvas

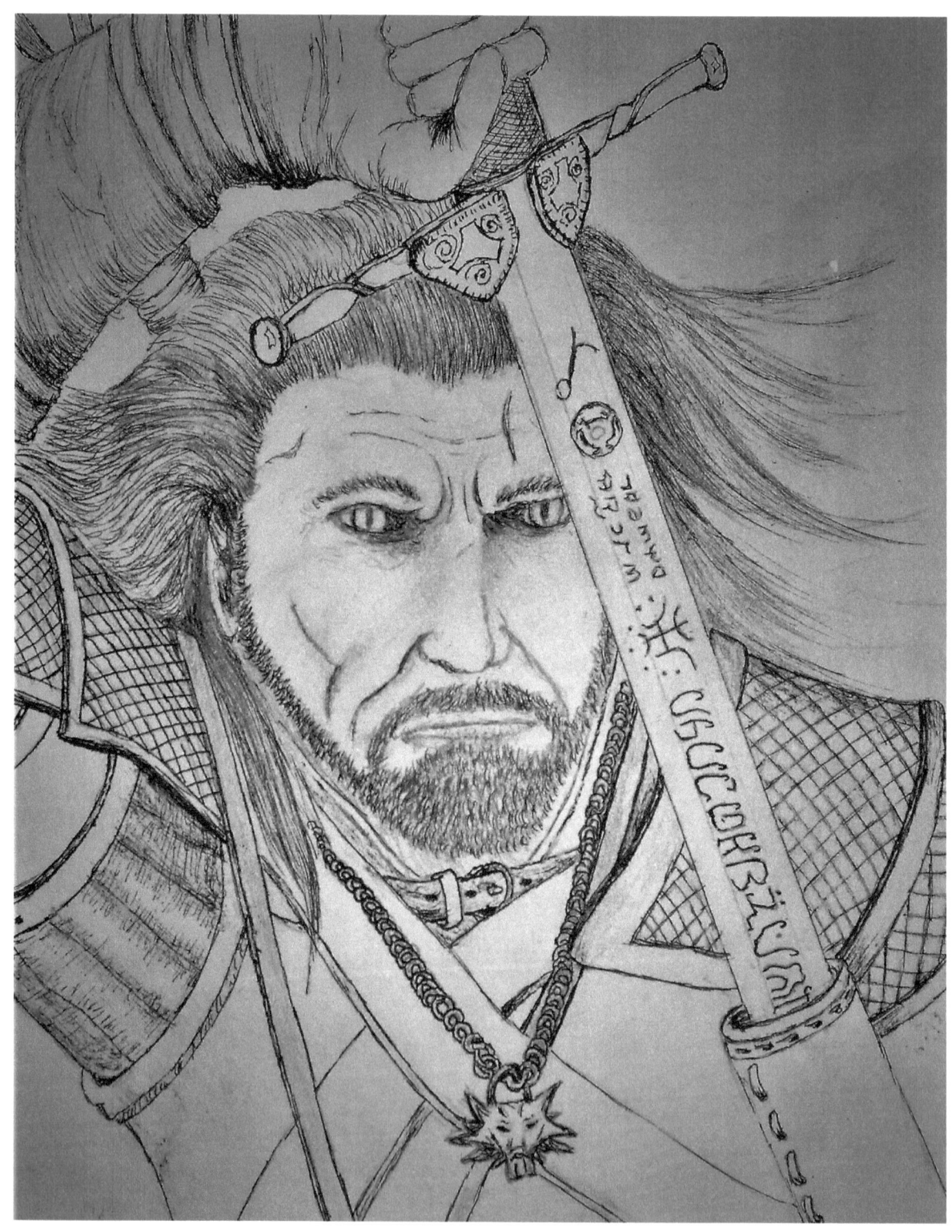

The Witcher

Ink on #100 paper

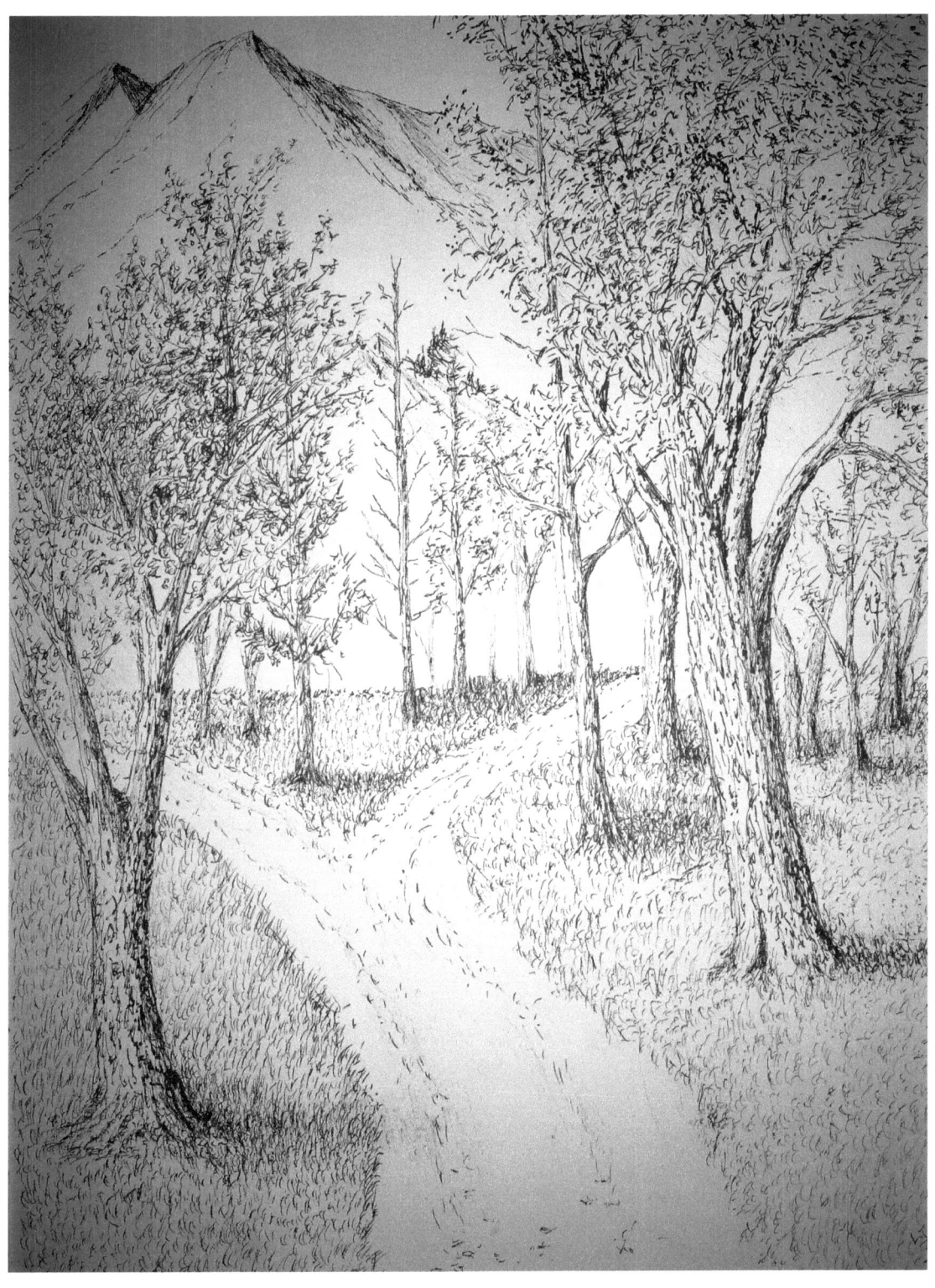

Divergence

Ink on #100 paper

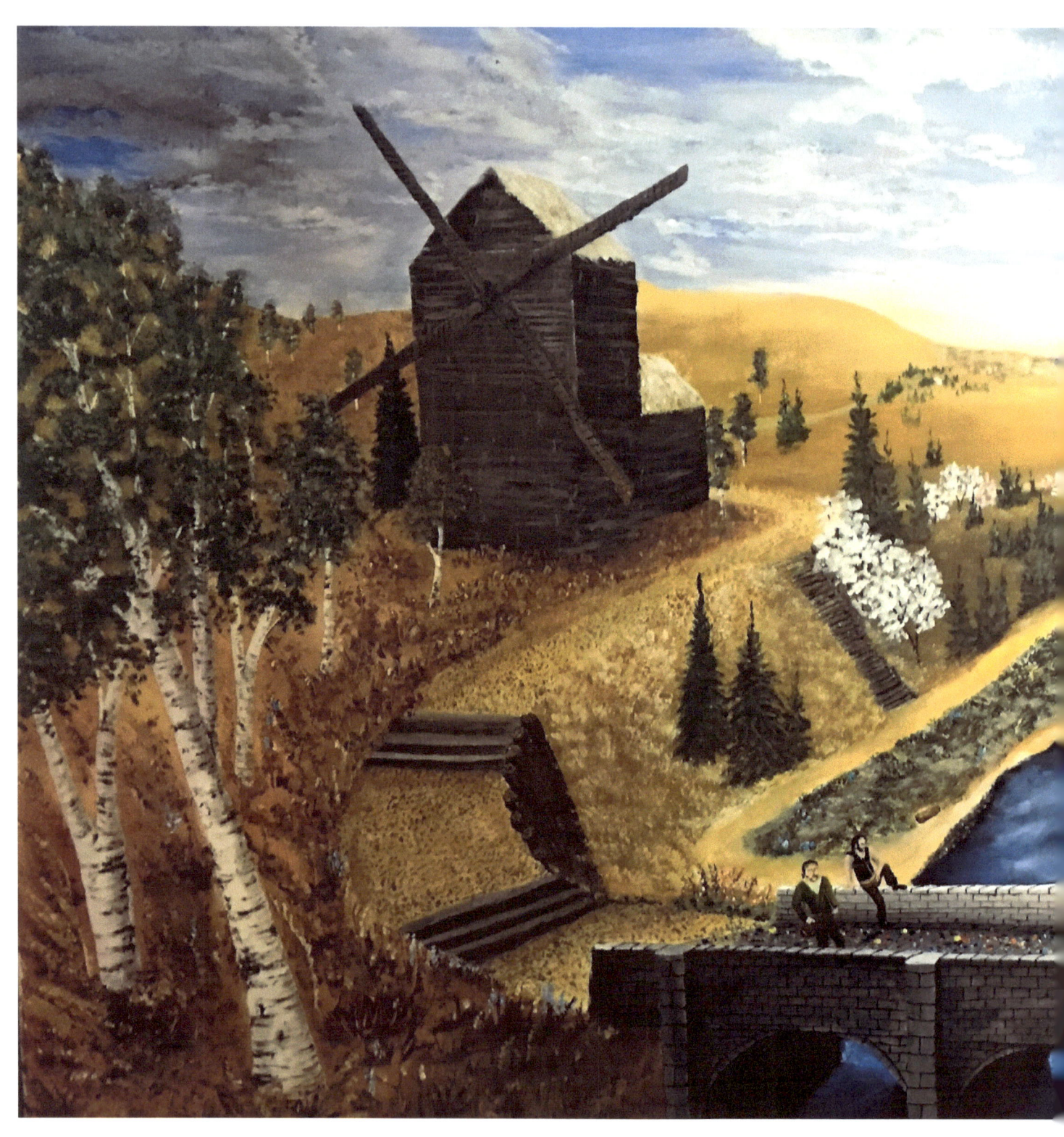

Wind in Scotland
Acrylic 50"x 20" stretched canvas

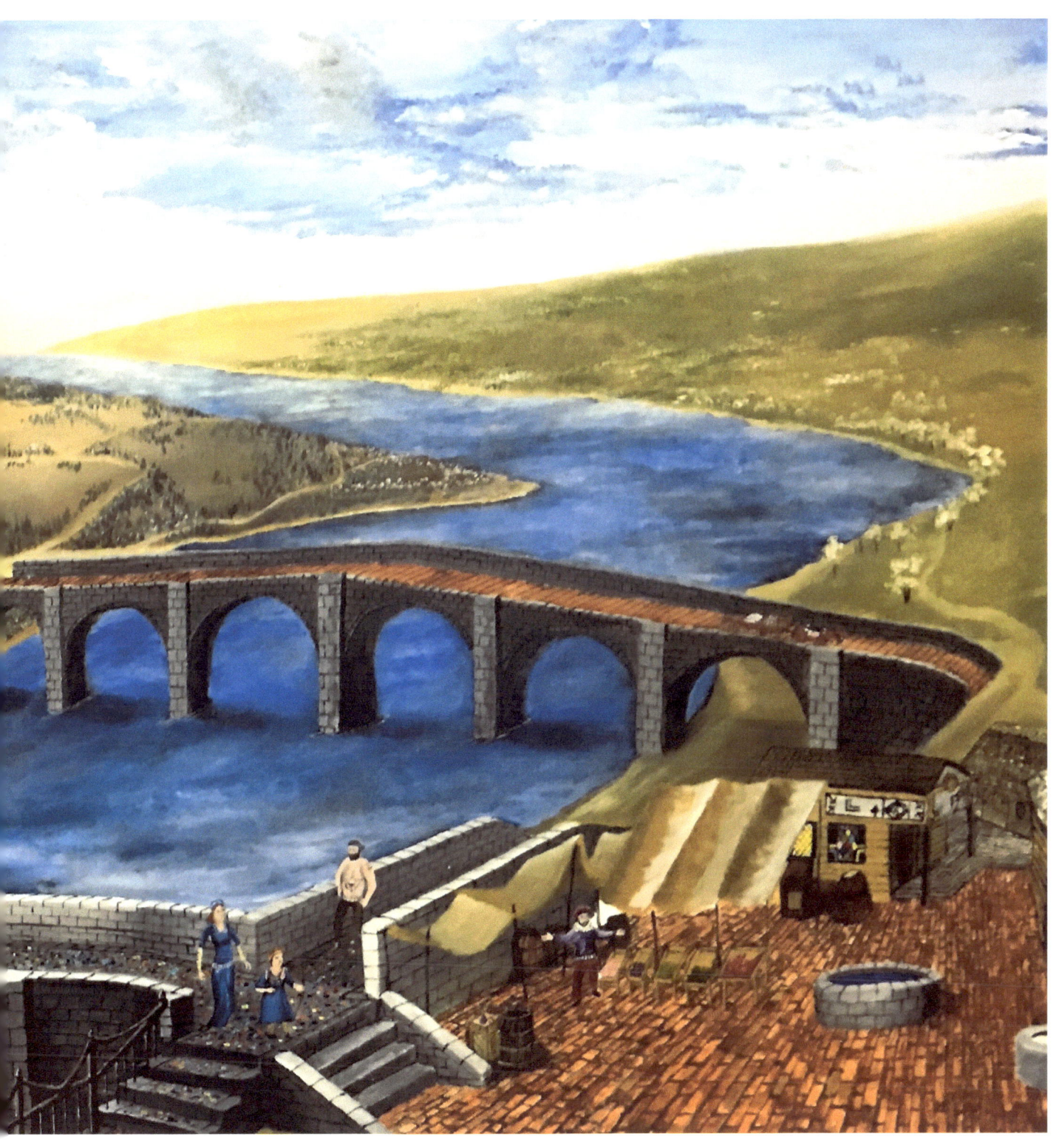

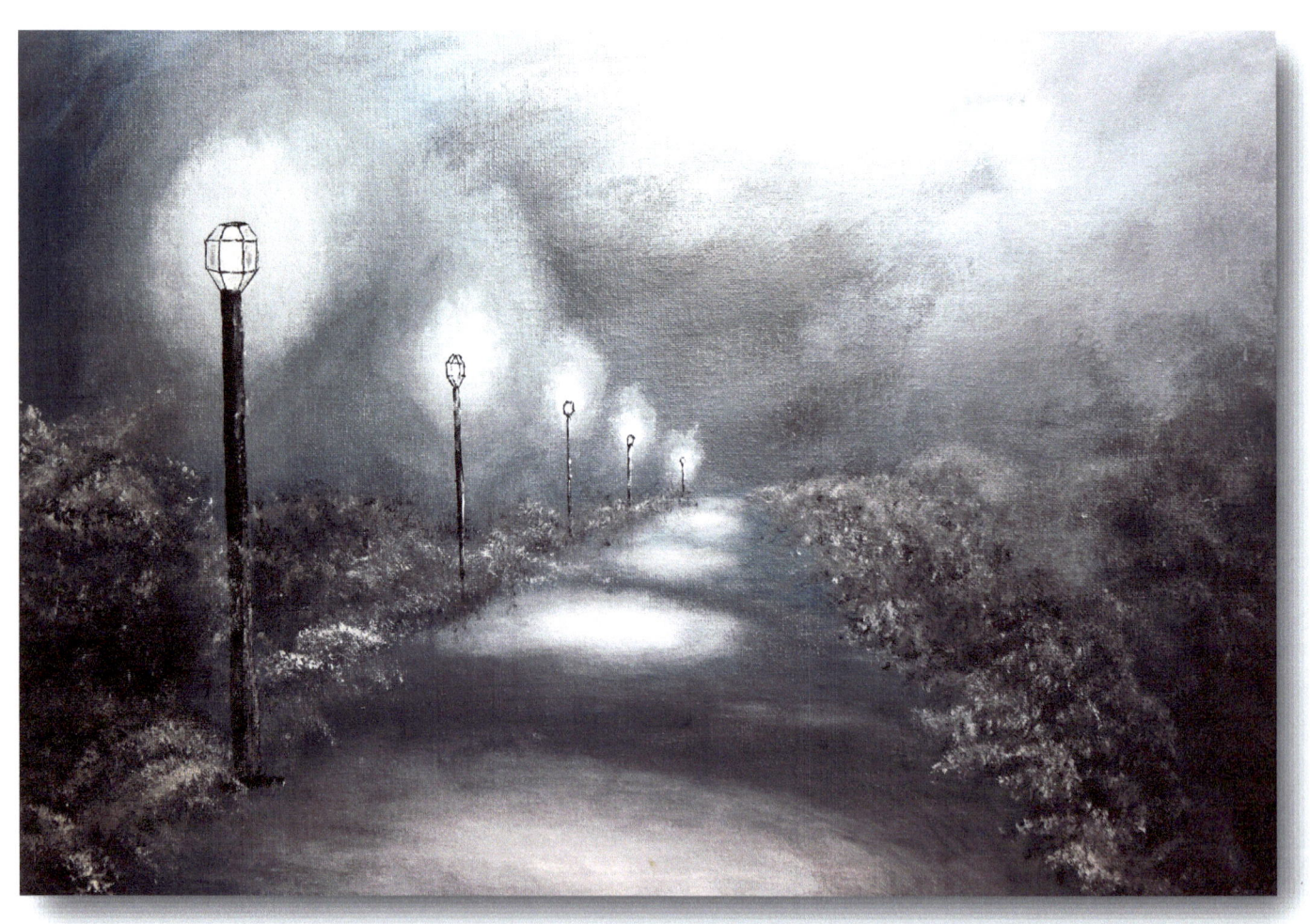

Shadows

Acrylic 16x20 panel board

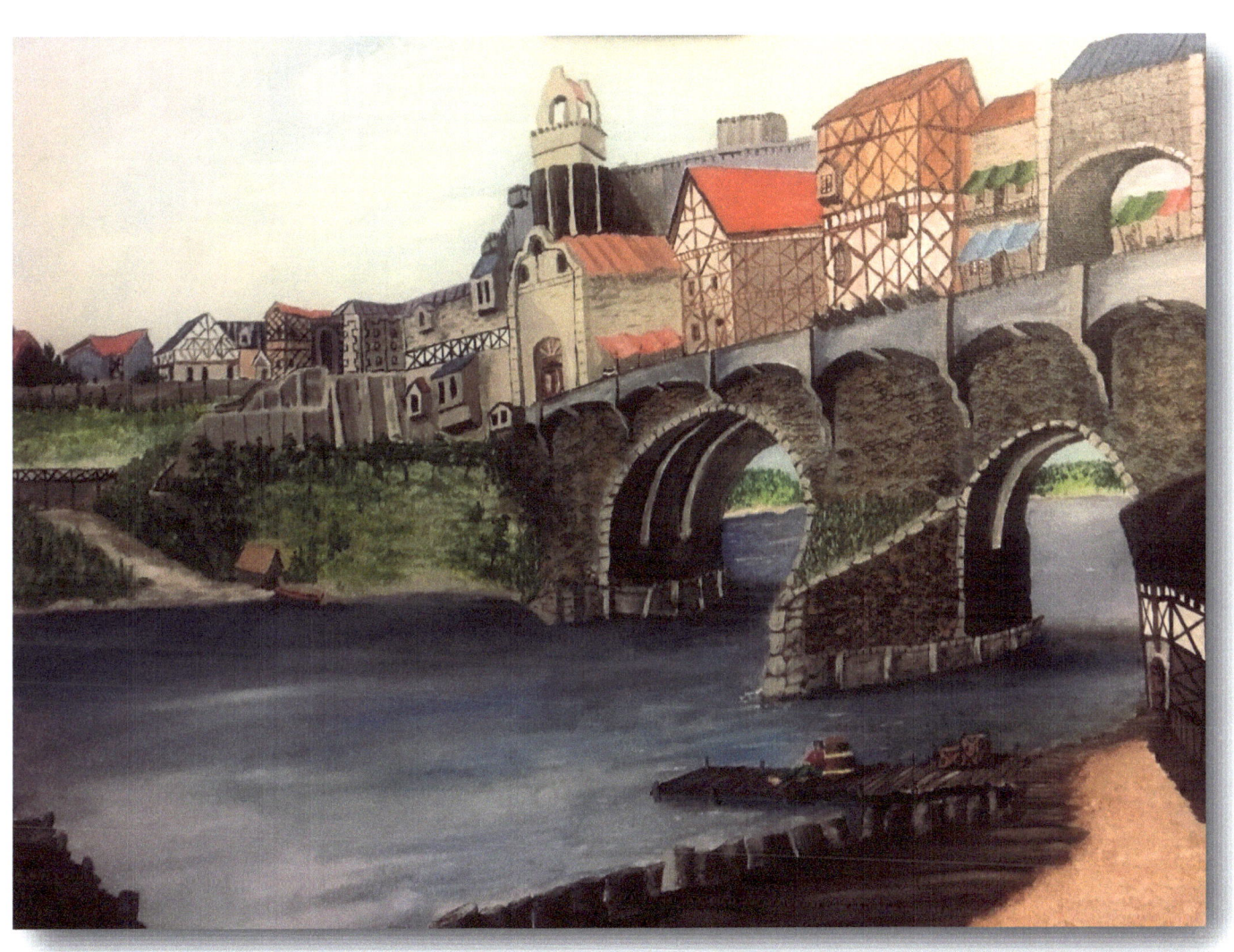

Dumbarton

16x20 stretched canvas print

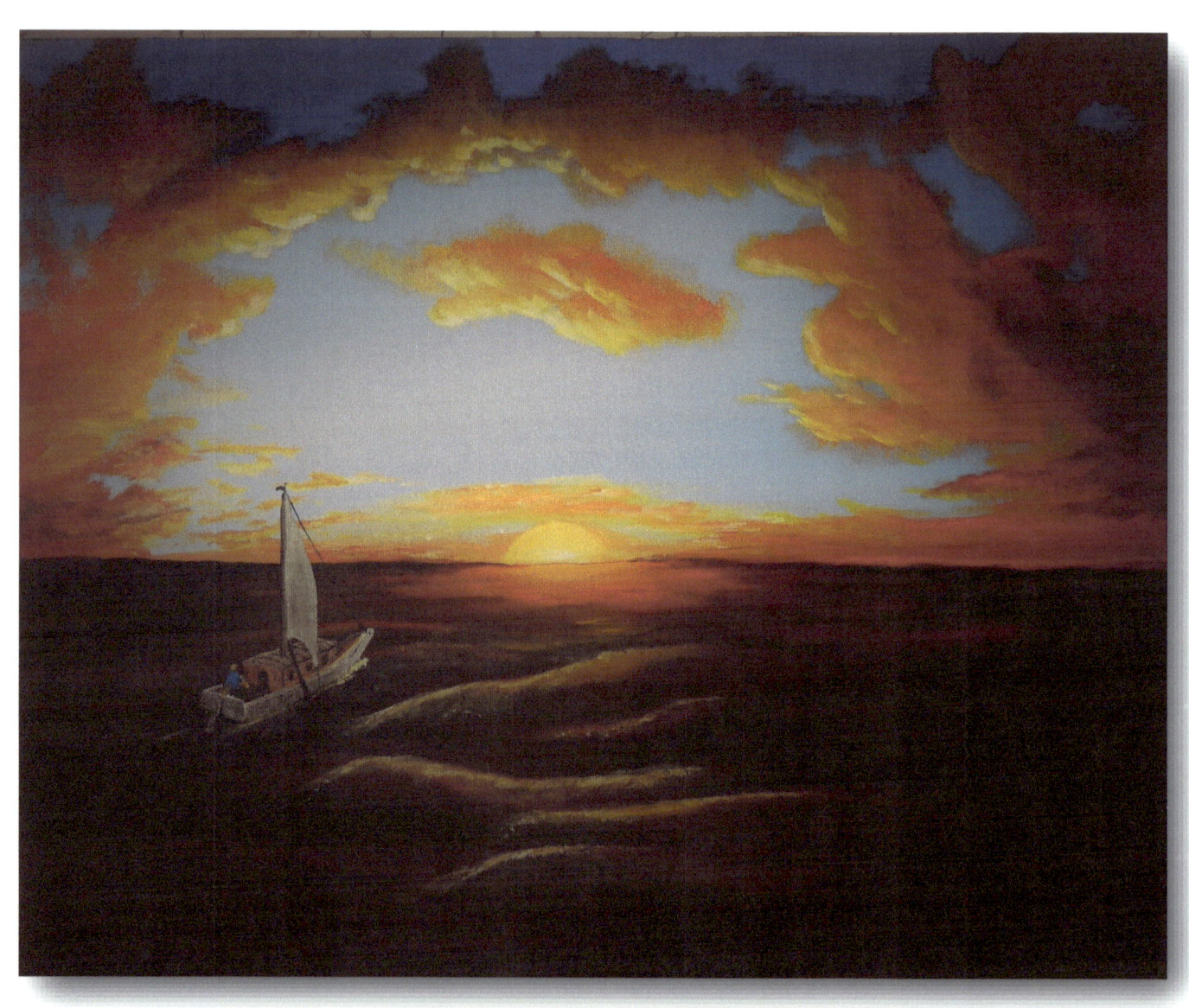

To Tomorrow

Acrylic 16x20 panel board

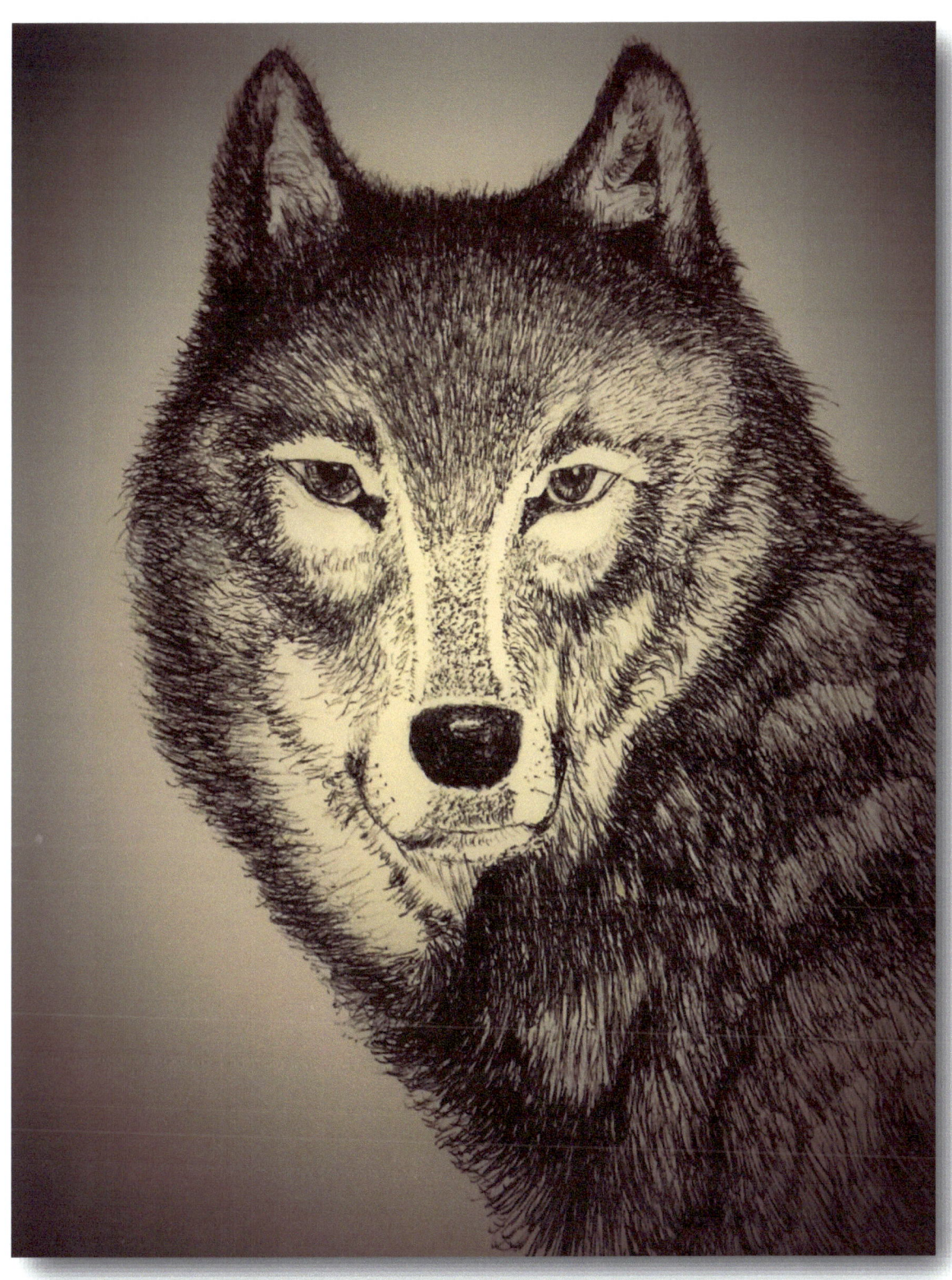

Wolf's Call

Ink 8x10 print #100 paper

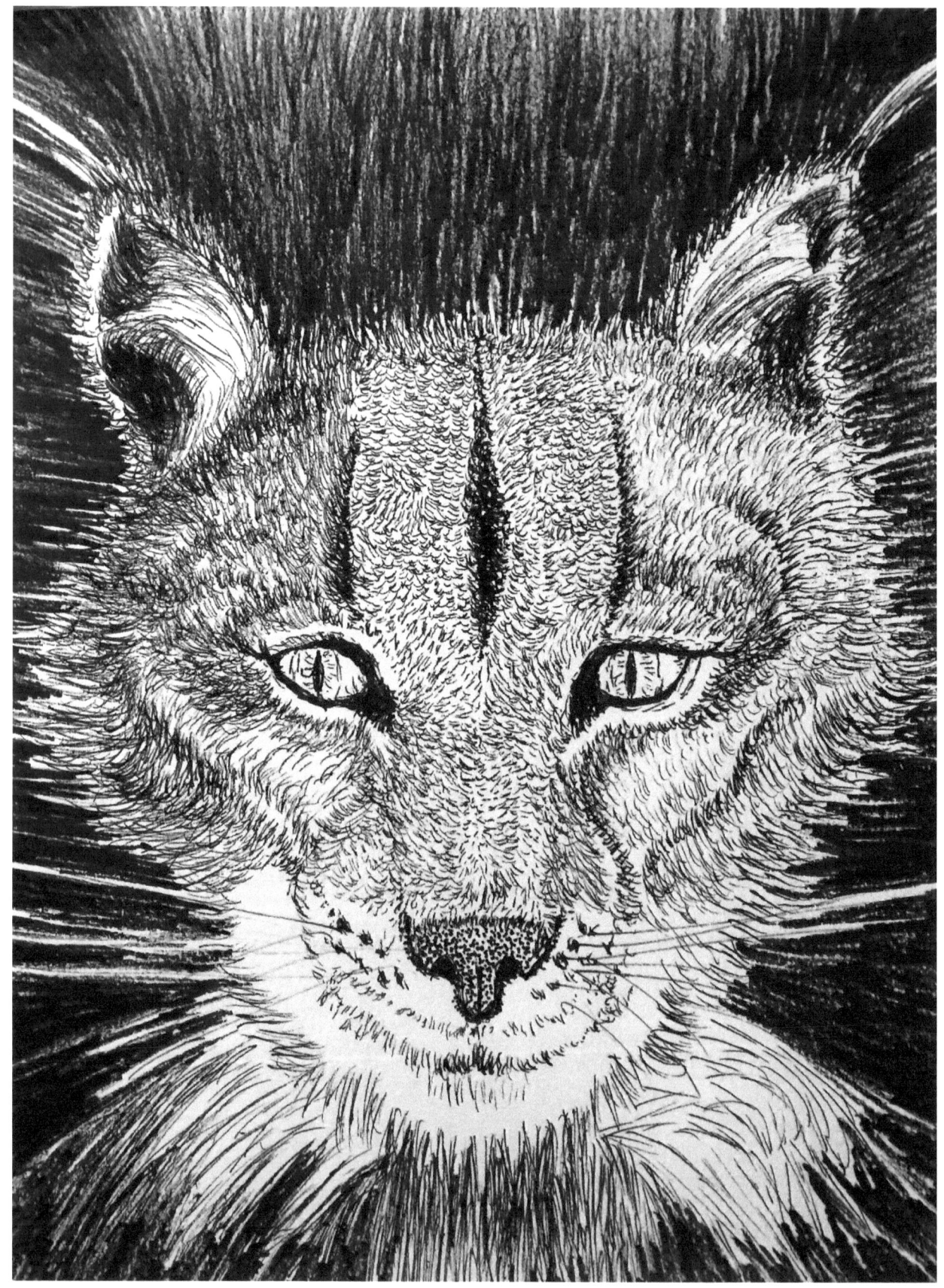

Transformation

Ink 8x10 #100 paper print

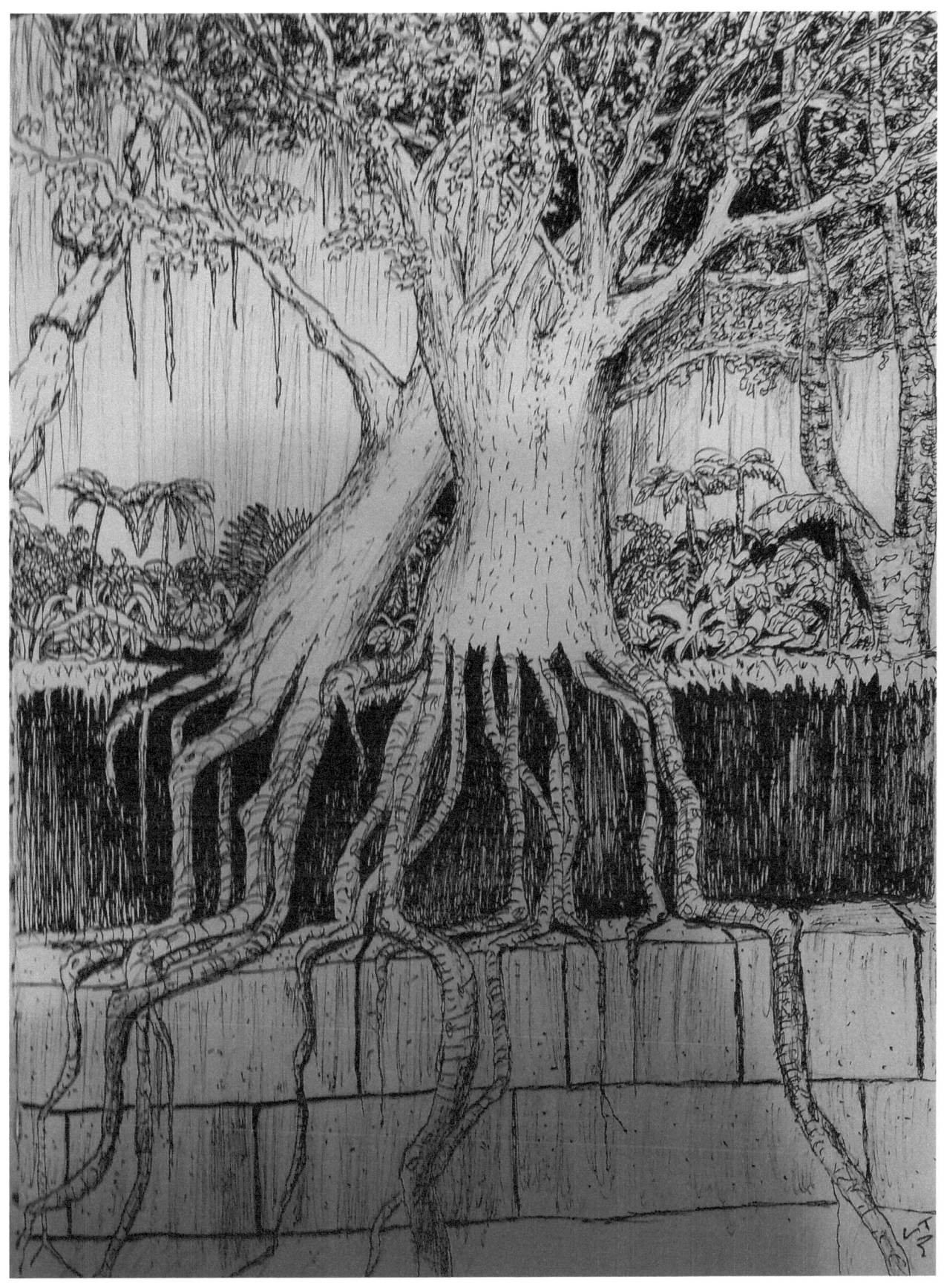

Consumed

Ink 8x10 #100 paper print

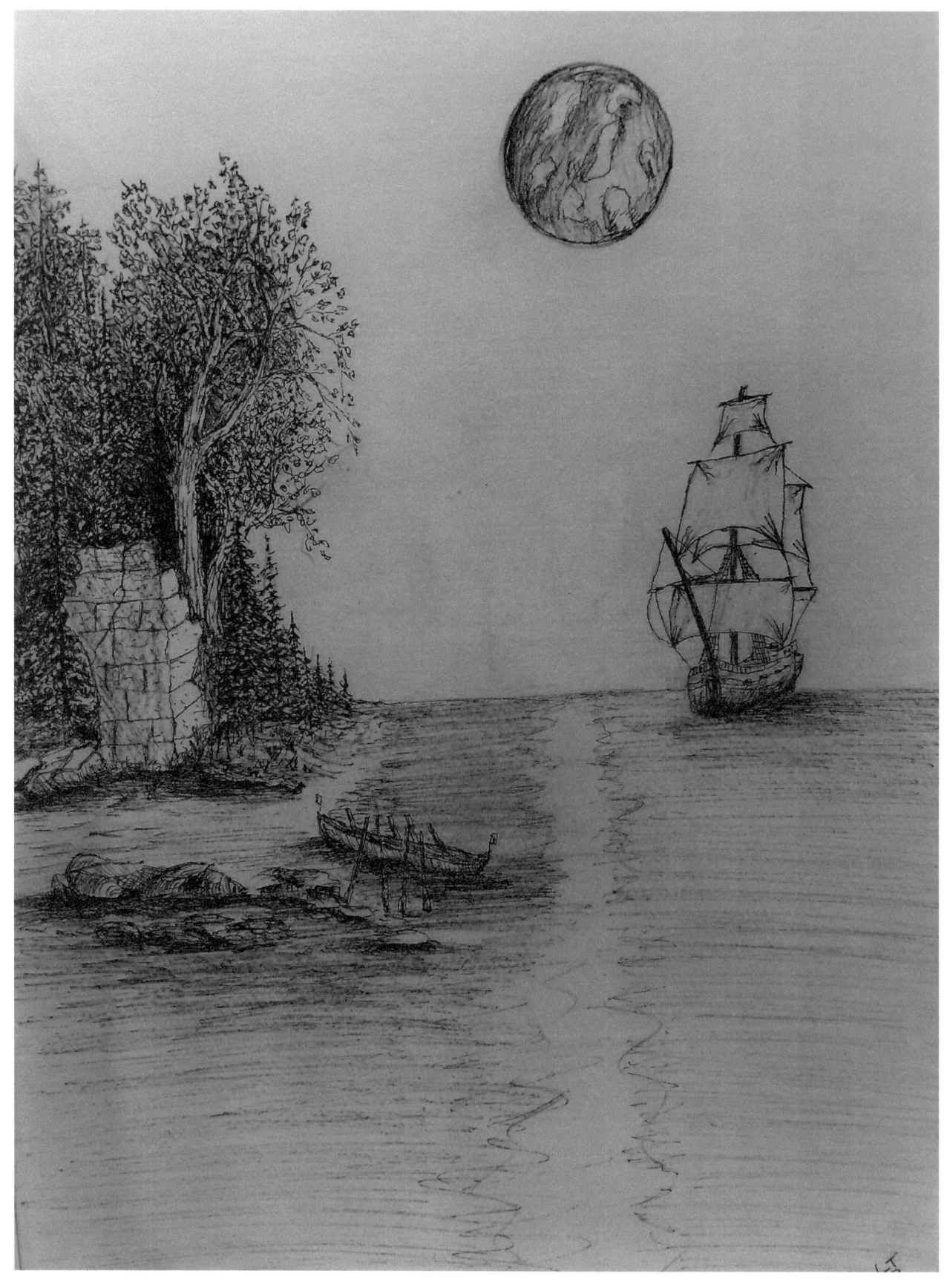

The Bonny

Ink 11x14 #100 paper print

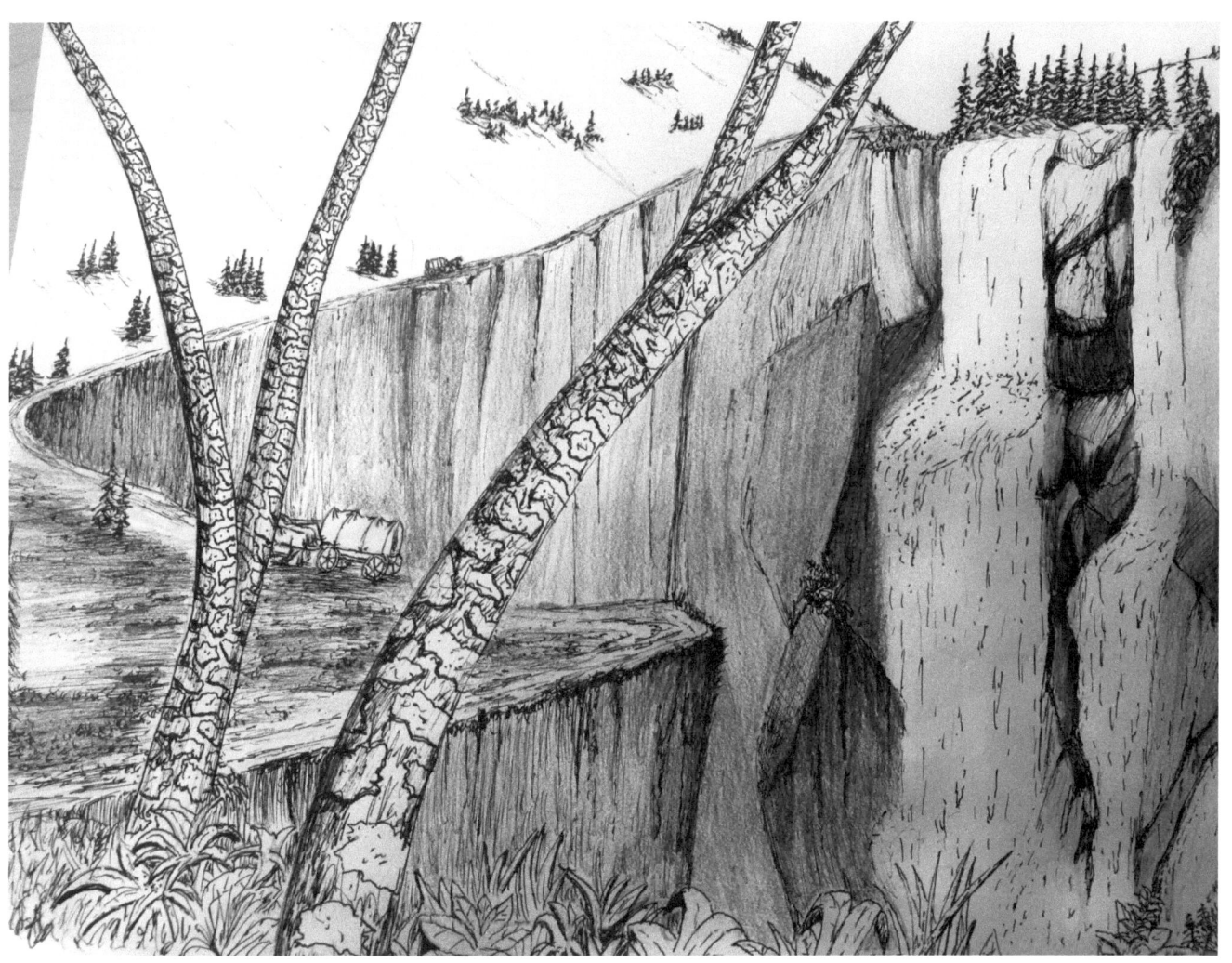

Wagon Train

Ink 11x14 #100 paper print

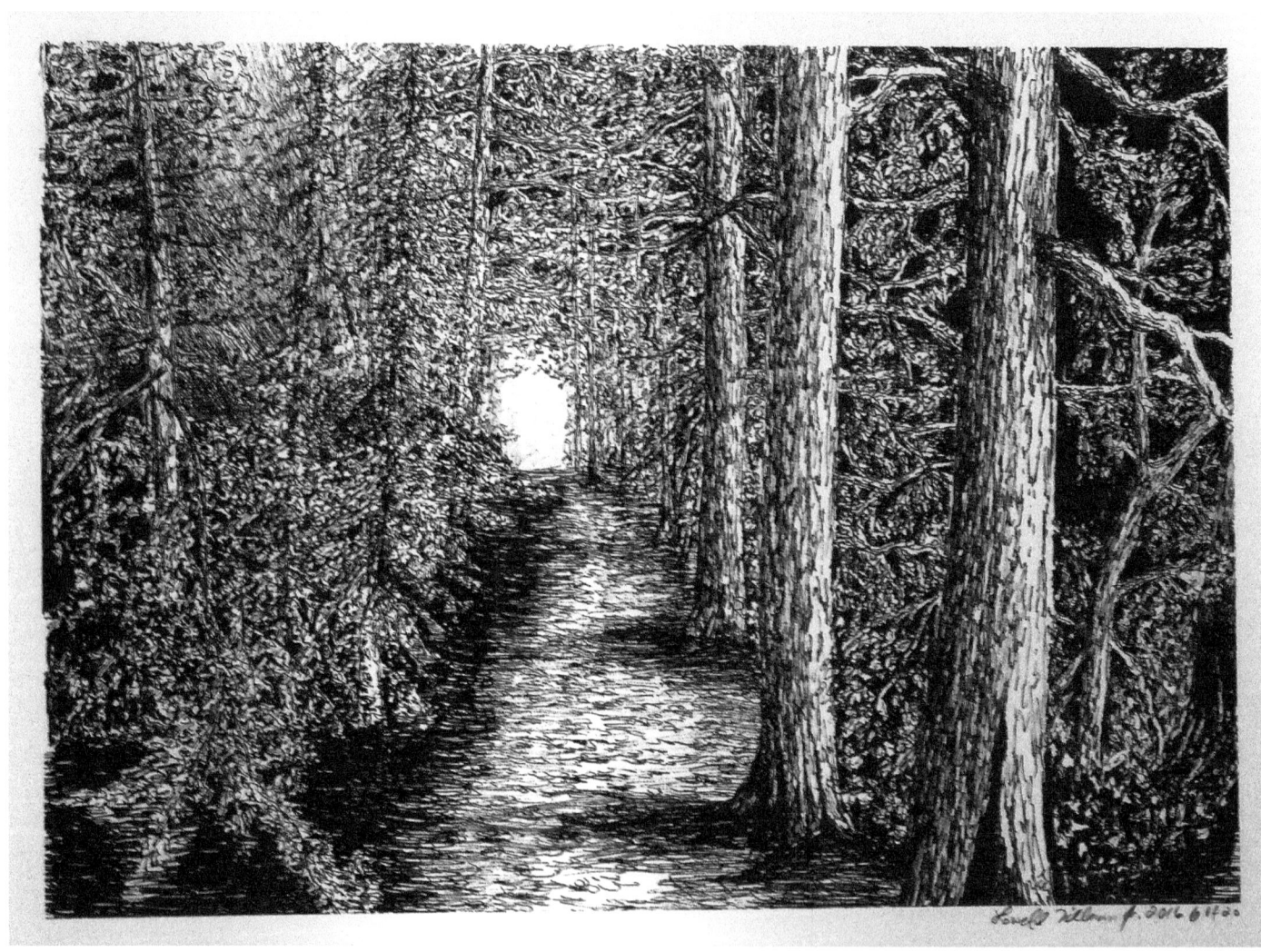

The Black Forest

Ink 11x14 #100 paper print

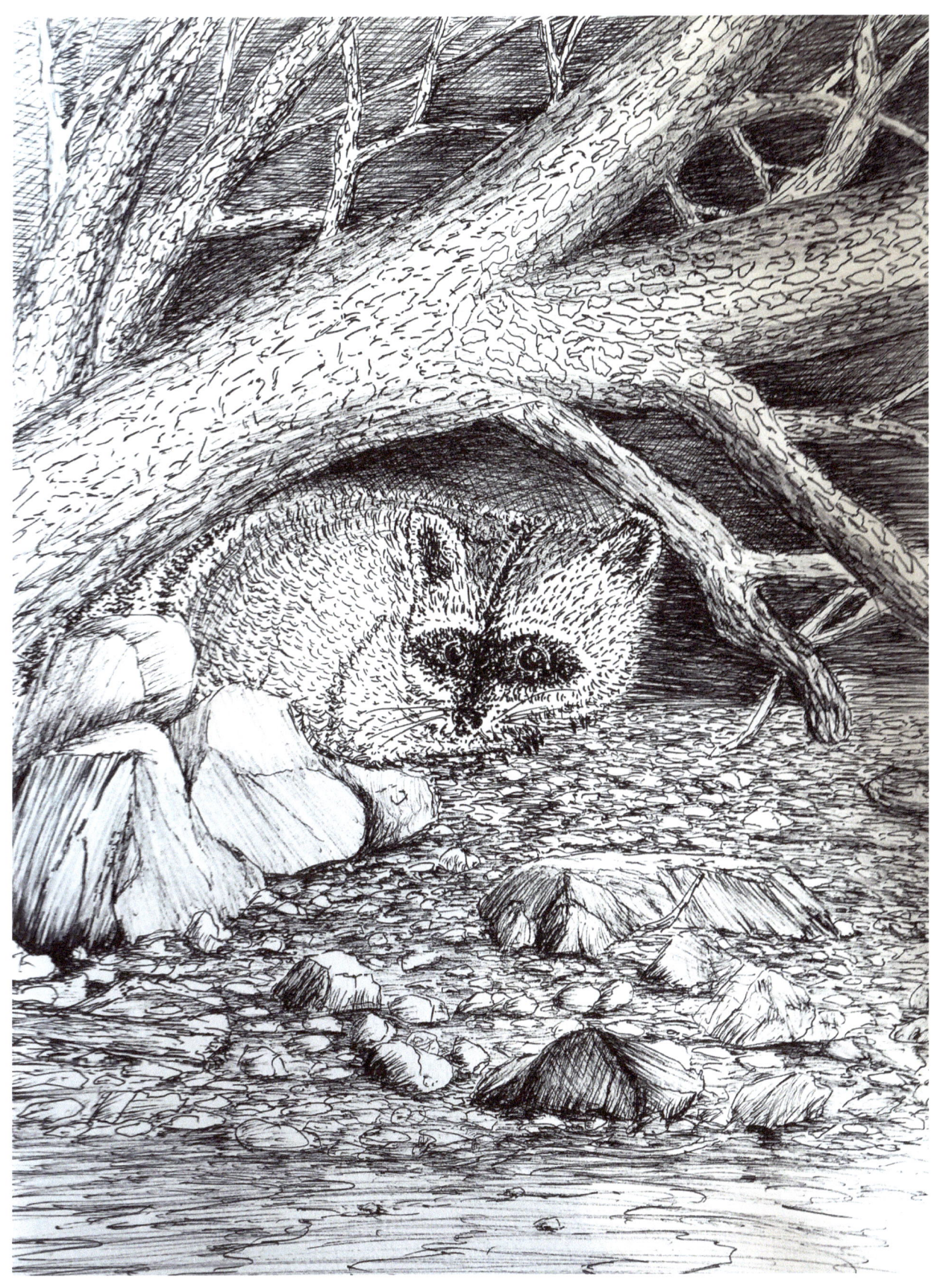

Shy Racoon

Ink 11x14 #100 paper print

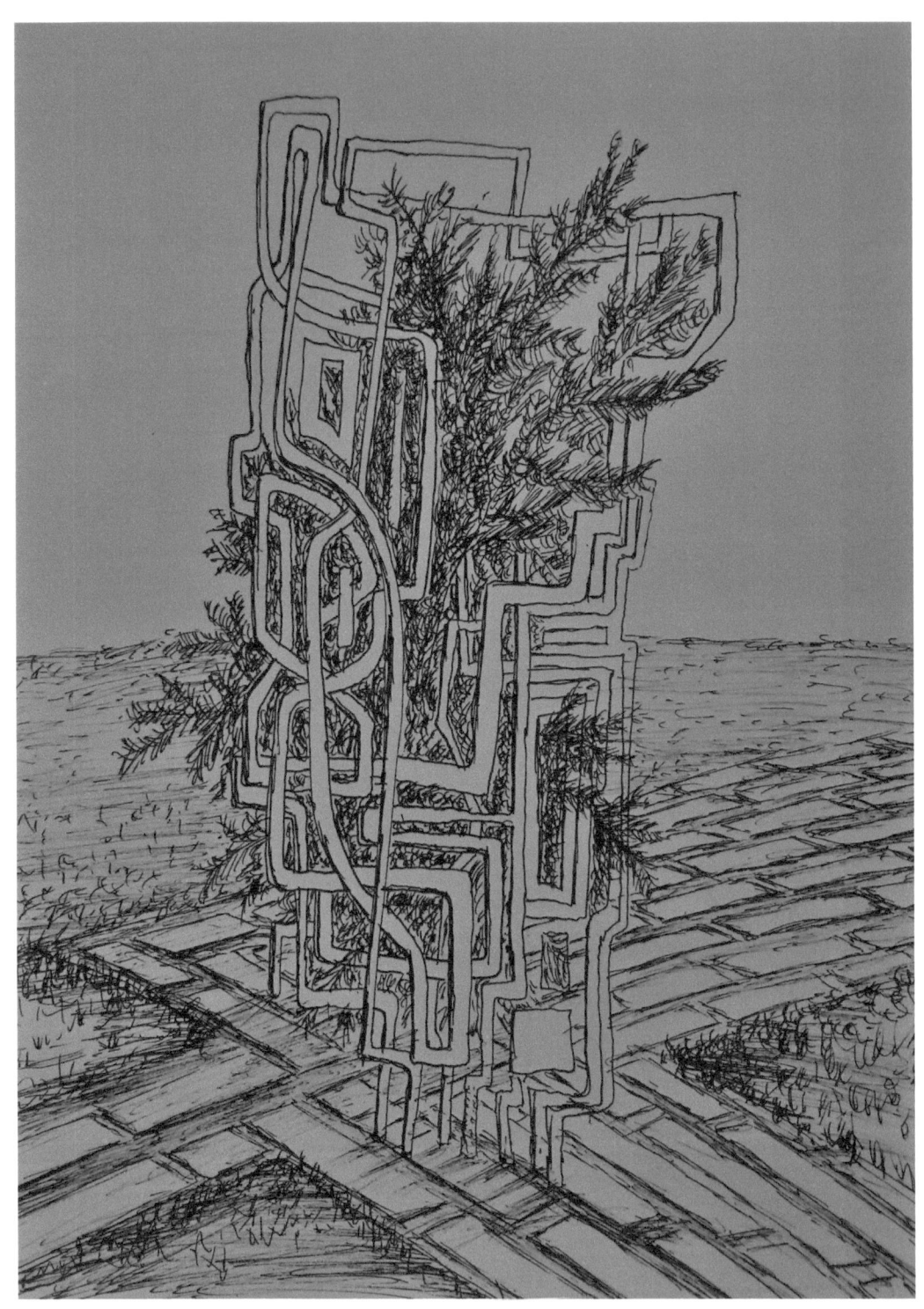

Trapped or Protected

Ink 11x14 #100 paper print

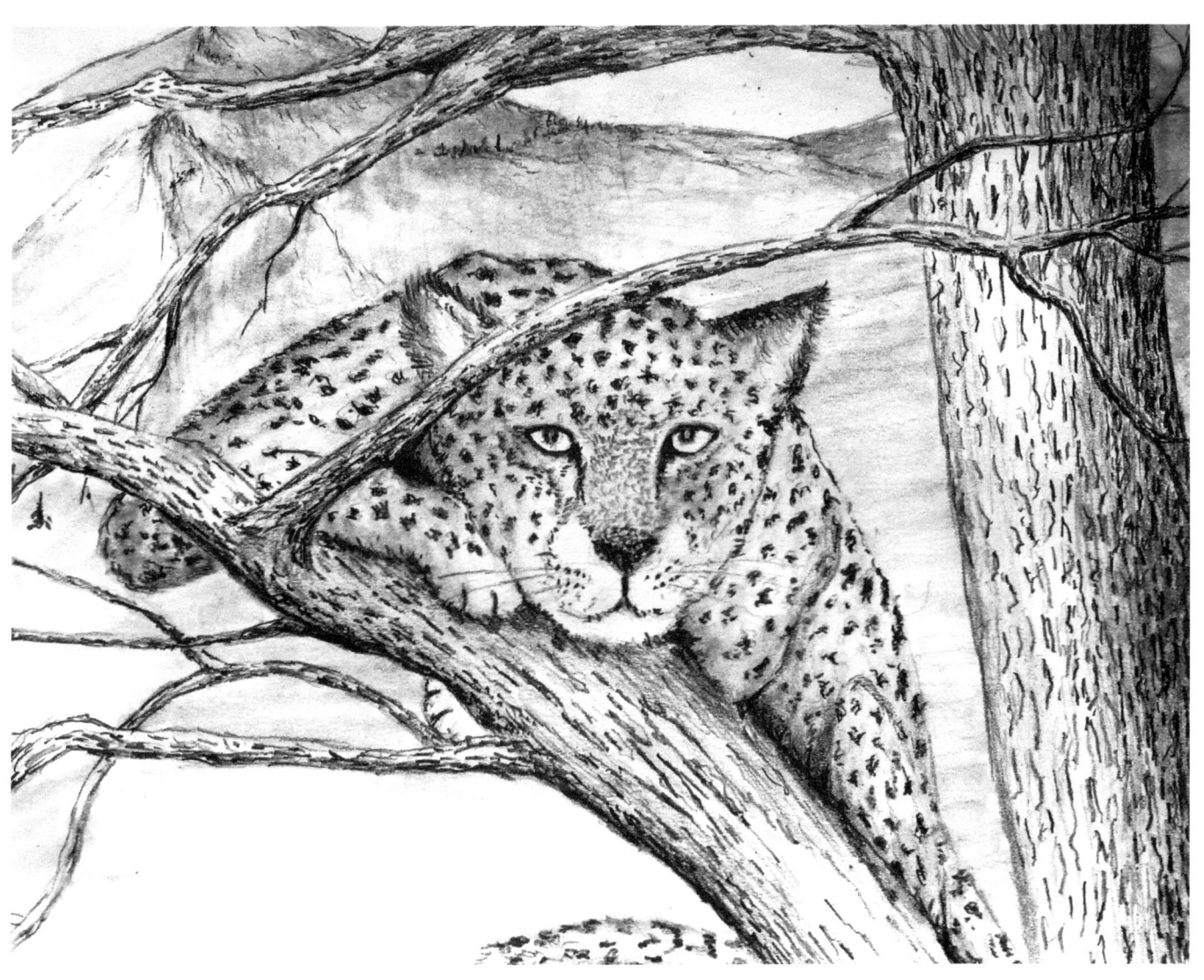

Precious

Ink 11x14 #100 paper print

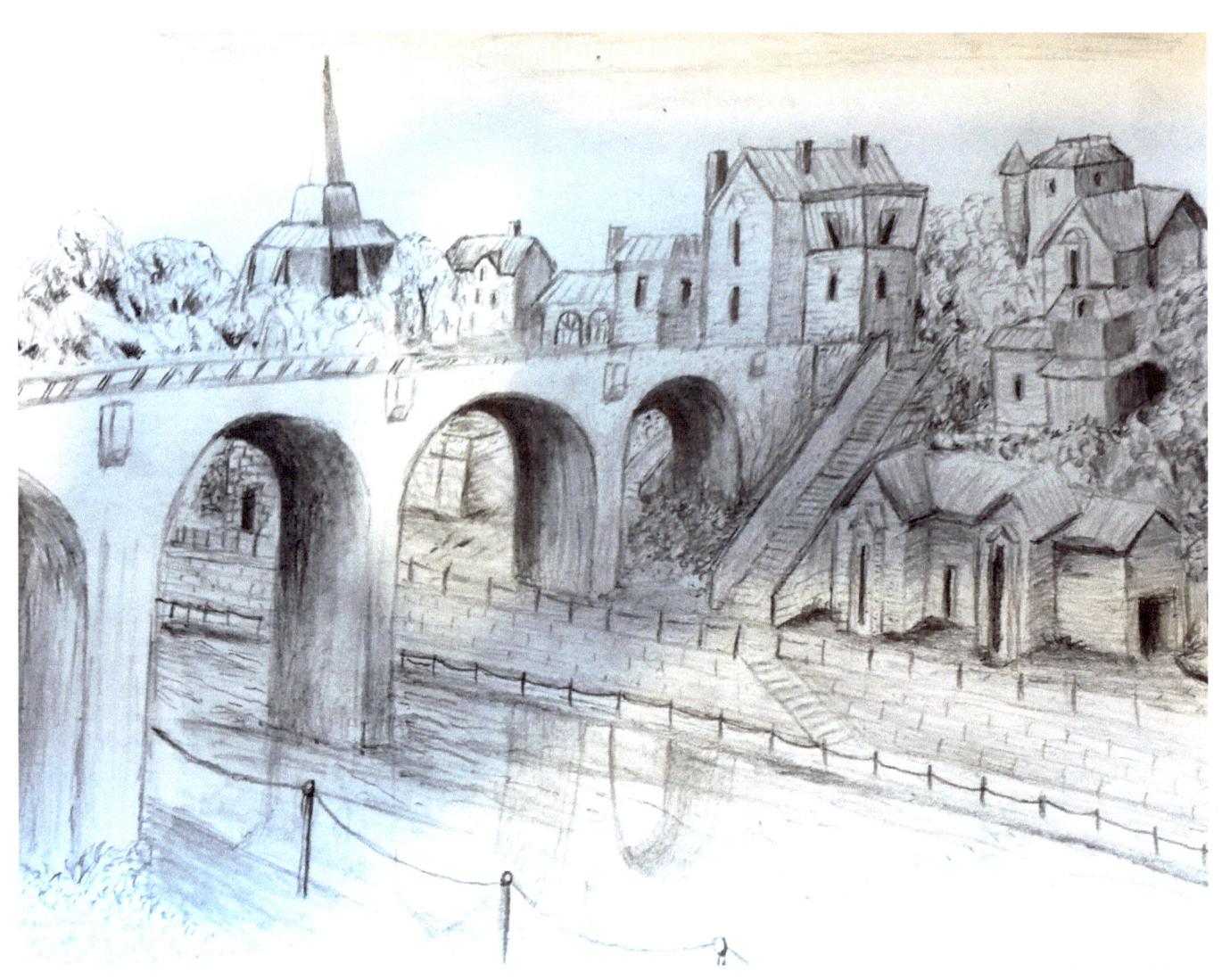

Amaryllis

Ink 11x14 #100 paper print

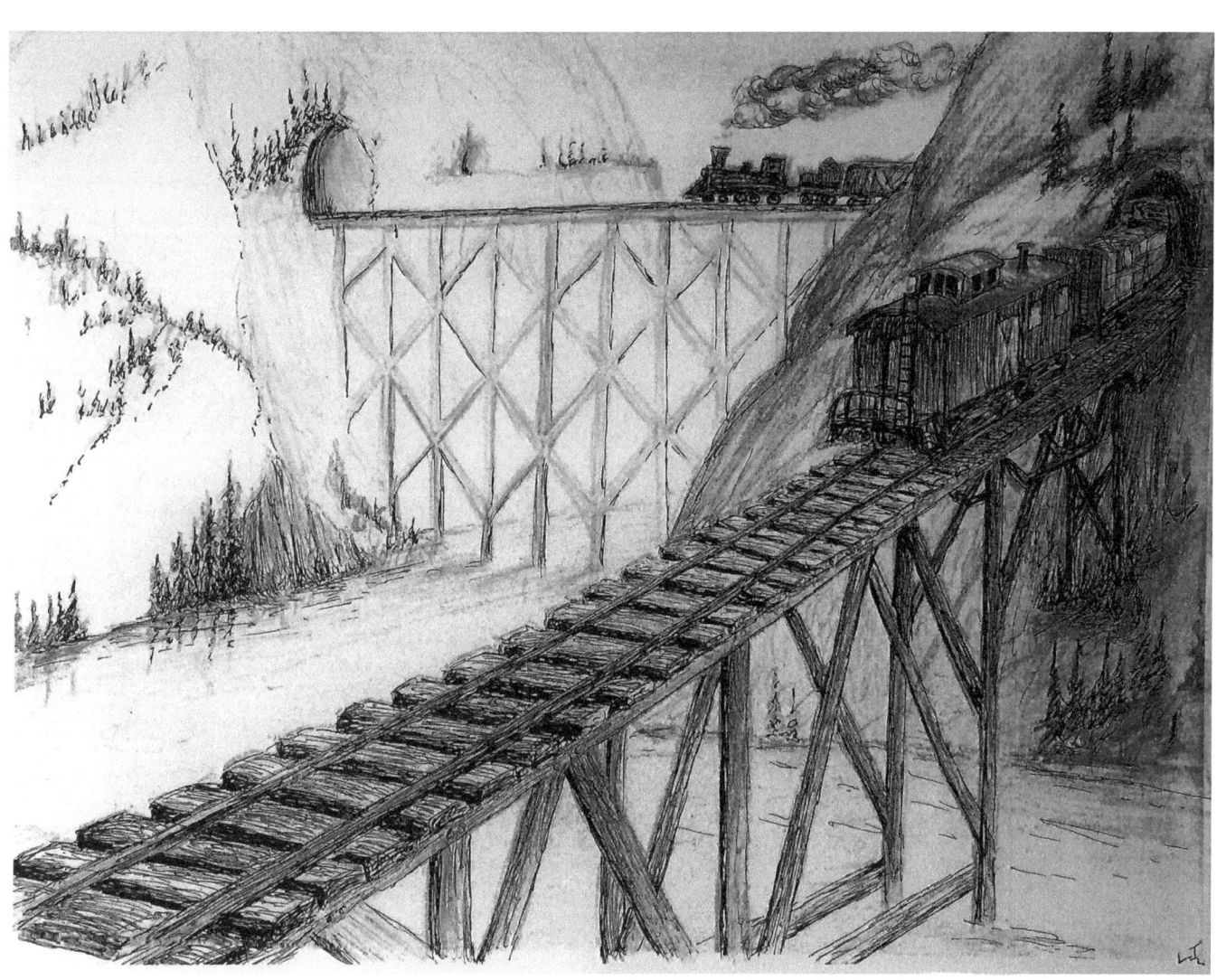

Number 9

Ink 11x14 #100 paper print

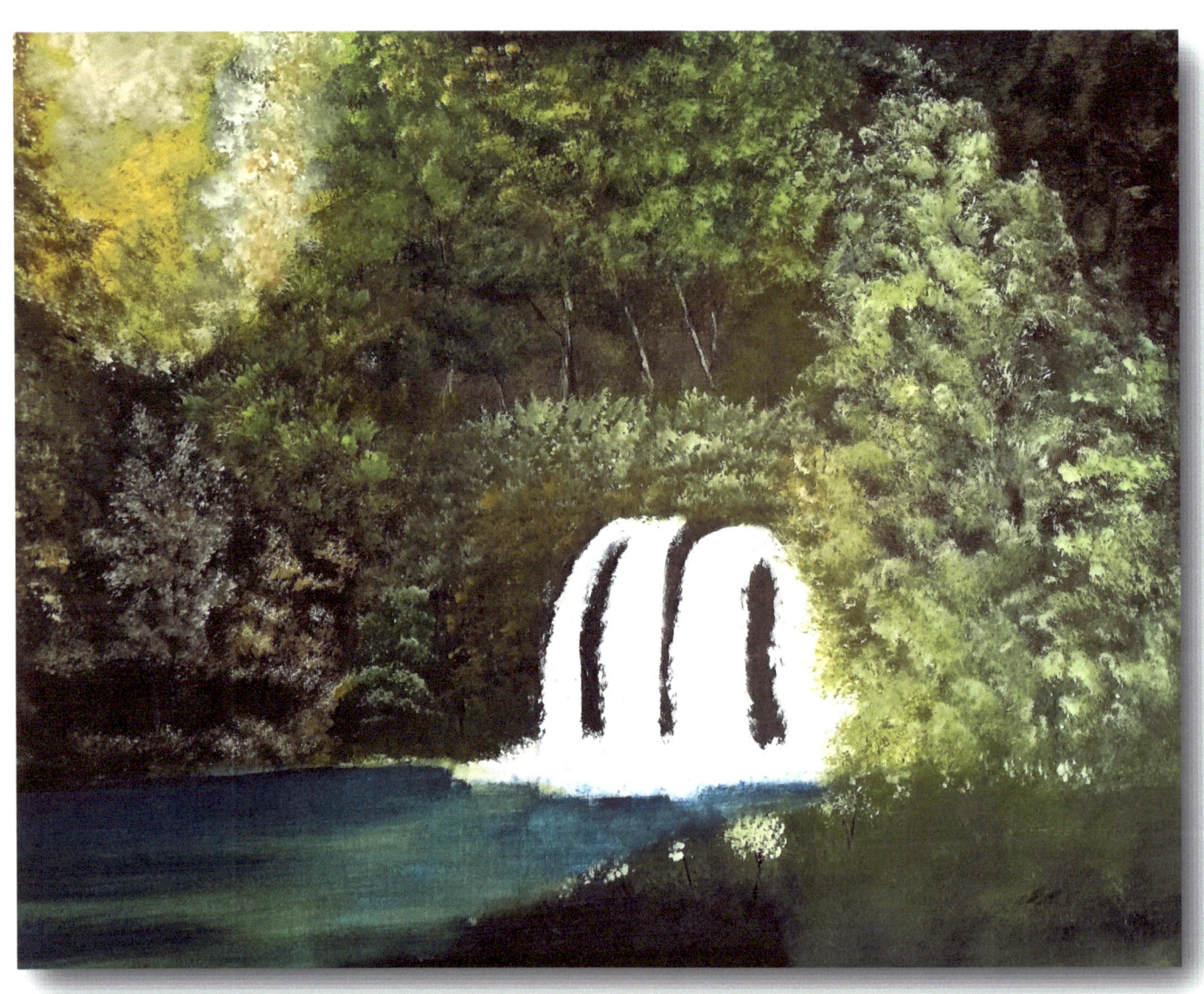

Jungle Falls

Acrylic 16x20 panel board

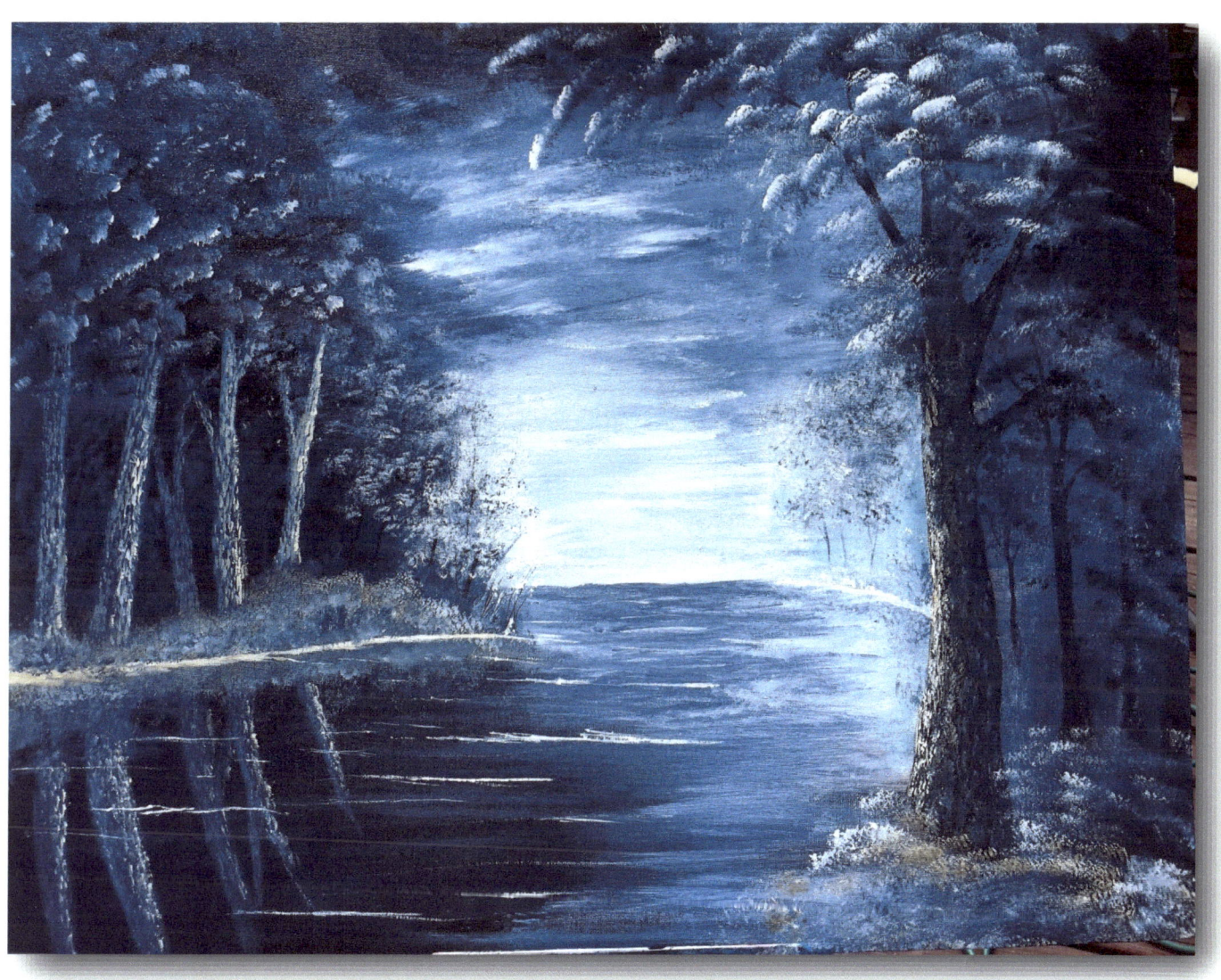

North

Acrylic 16x20 panel board

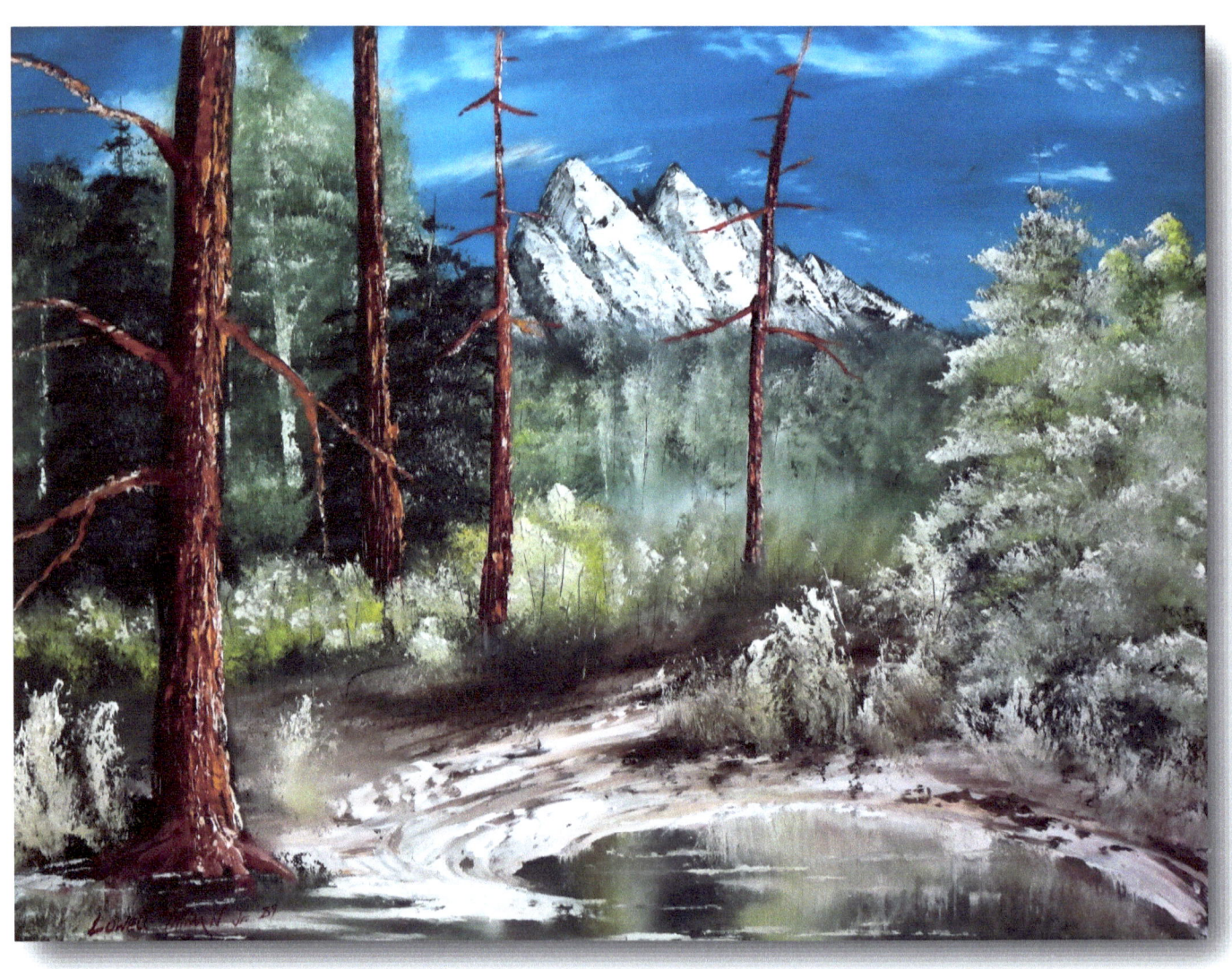

Cedar

Acrylic 16x20 panel board

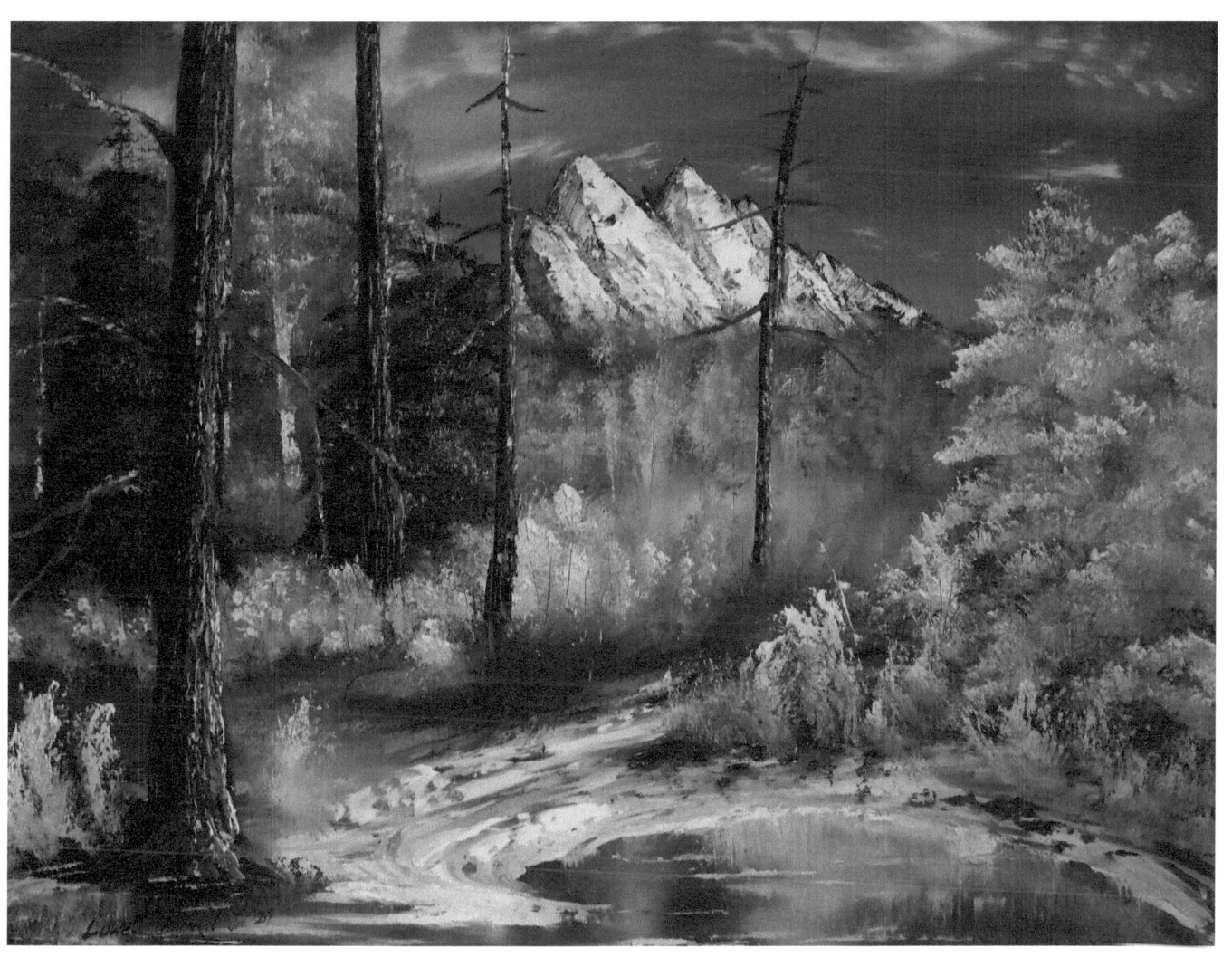

Cedar at Night

Acrylic 16x20 panel board print

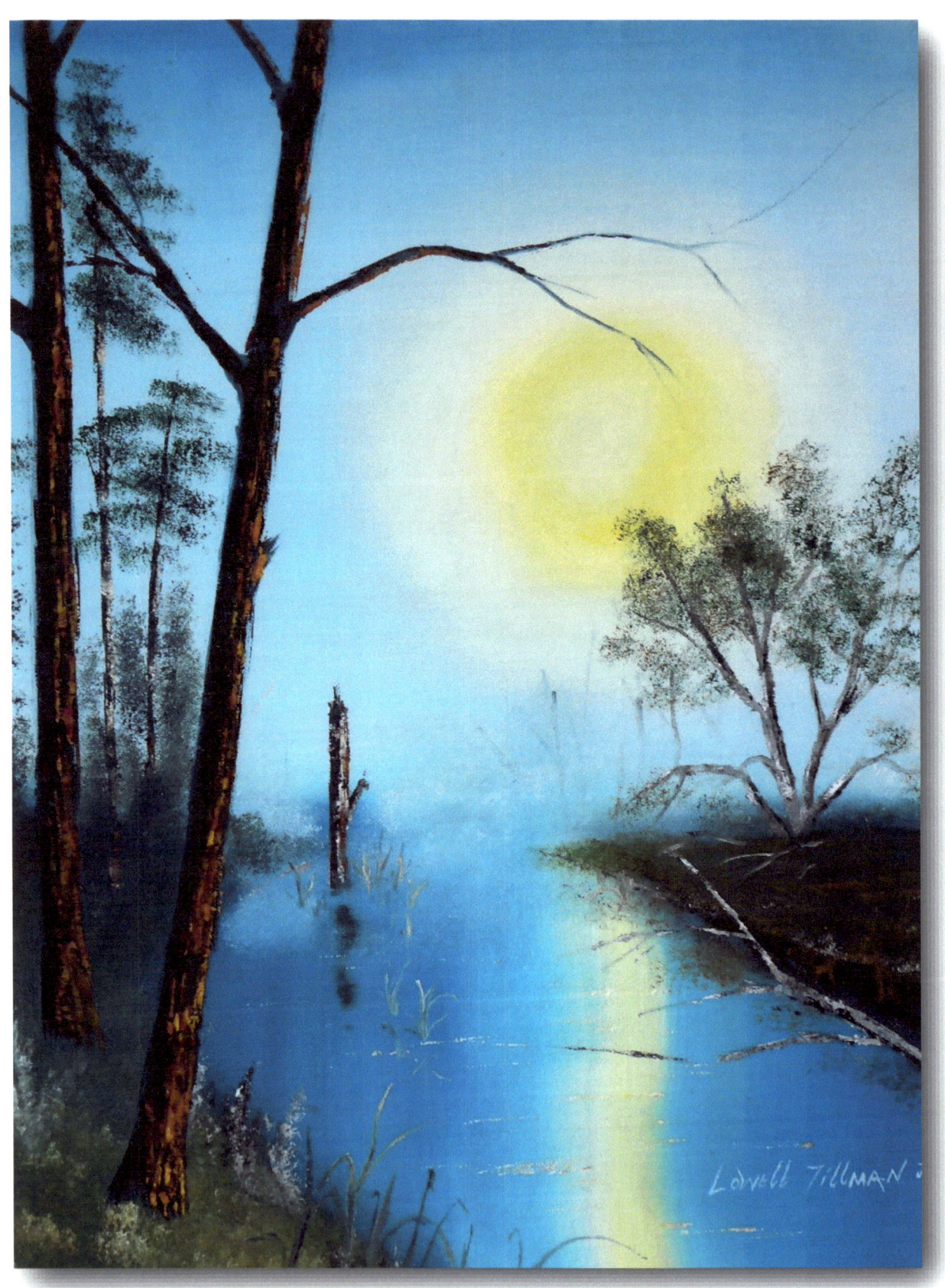

Moon Scape

Acrylic 16x20 panel board

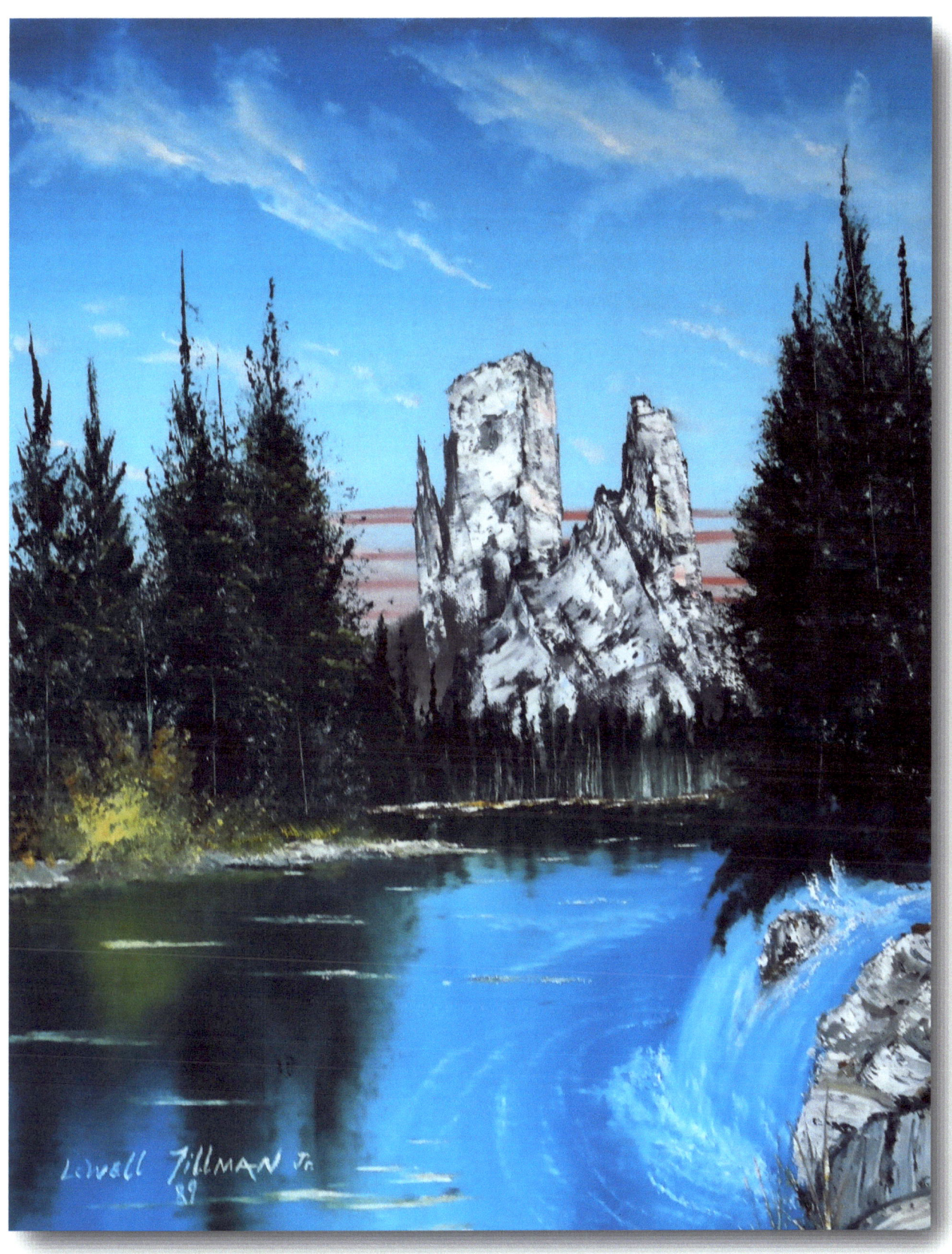

Broken Fall

Acrylic 16x20 panel board

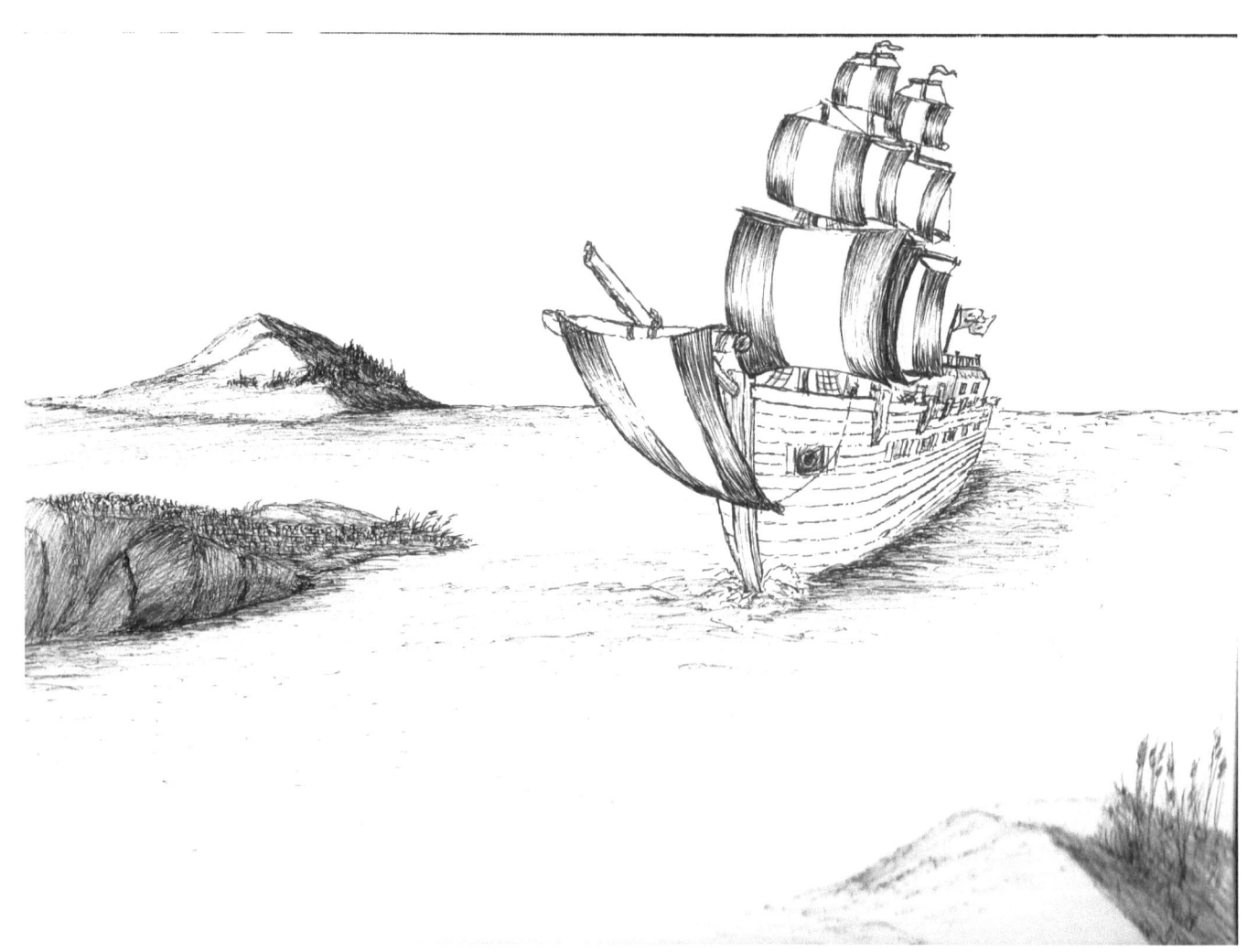

Crossing the Line

Ink 8x10 #100 Paper Print

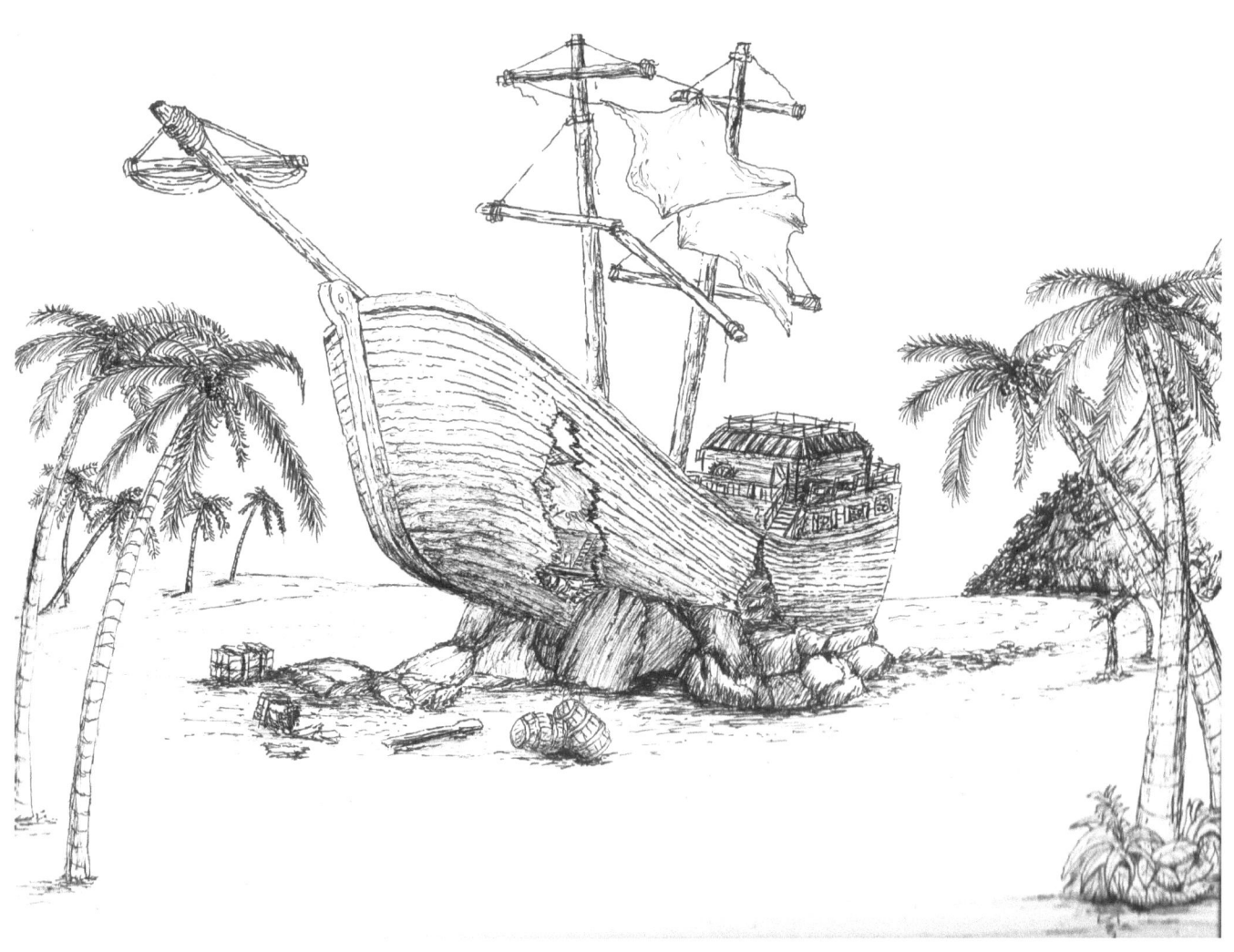

Marooned

Ink 8x10 #100 Paper Print

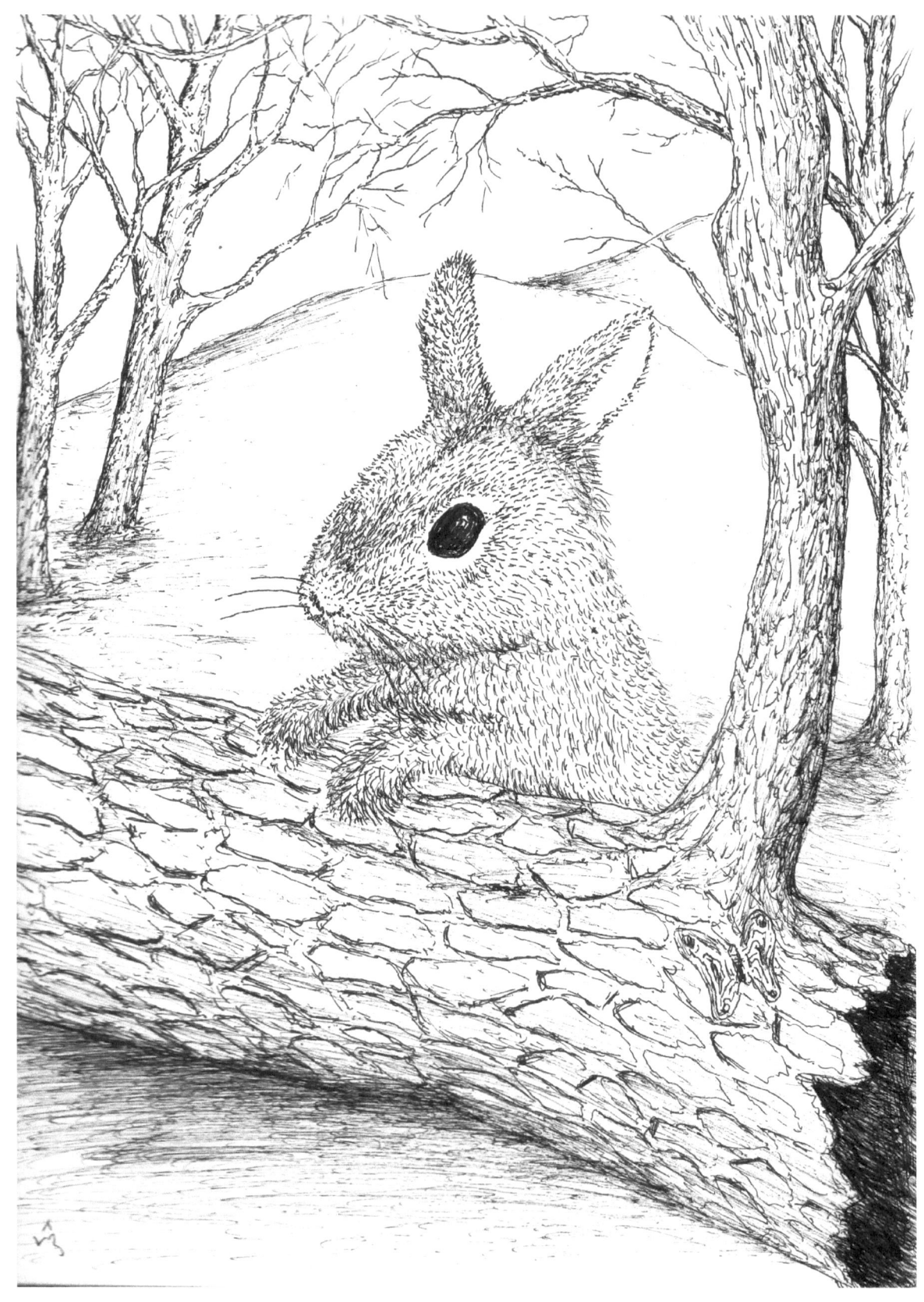

Fluffy

Ink 8x10 #100 Paper Print

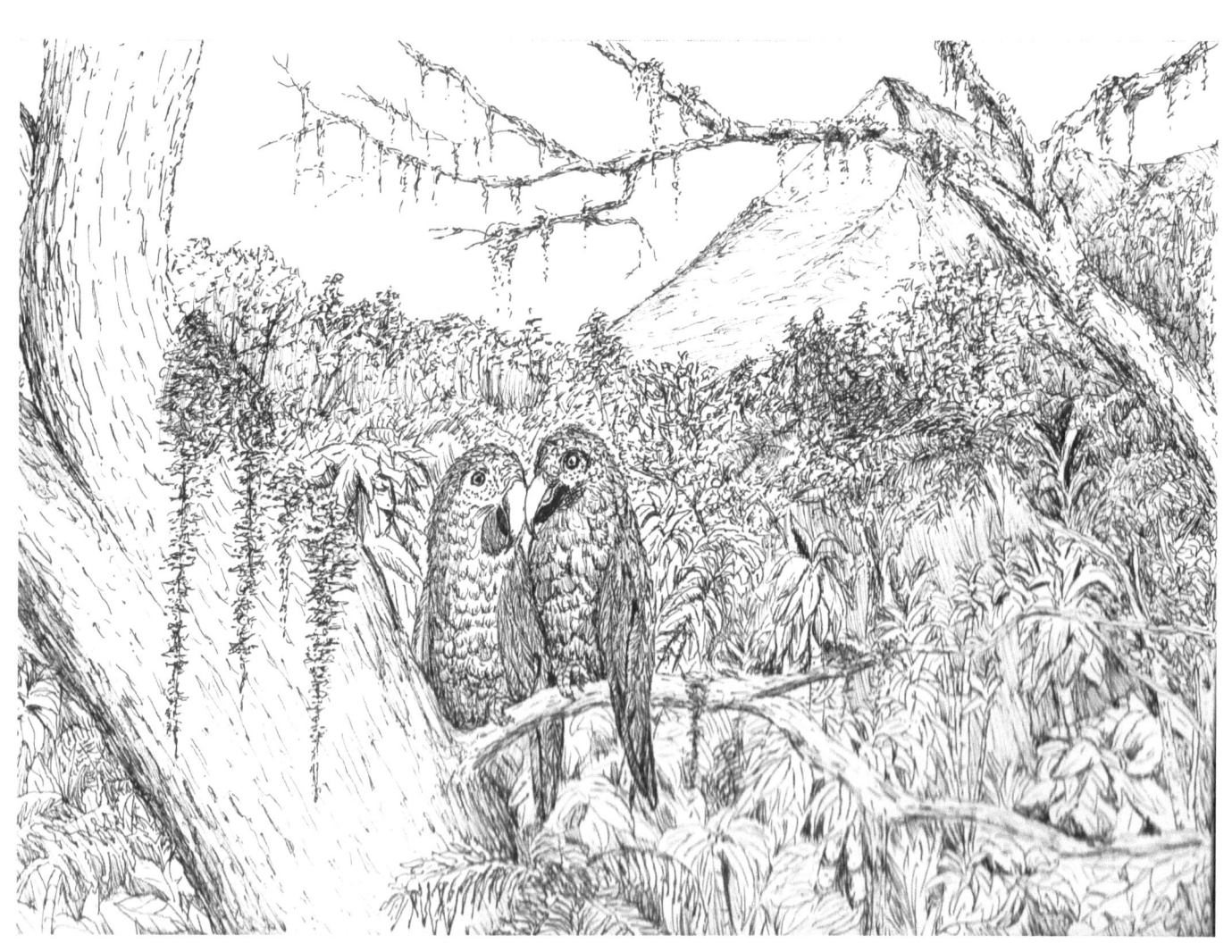

Lovers in Paradise

Ink 8x10 #100 Paper Print

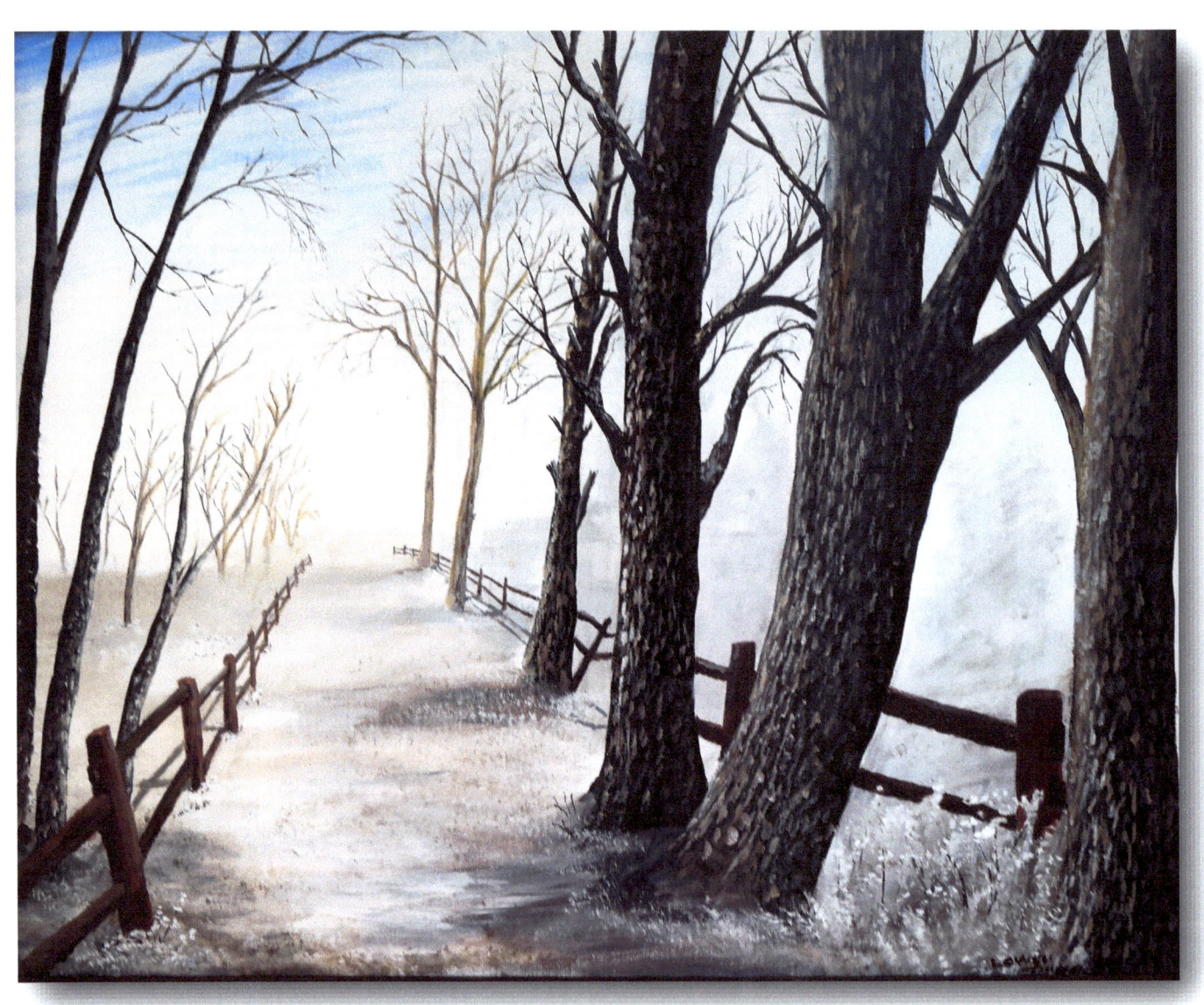

Minstrel Lane

Acrylic 16x20 panel board

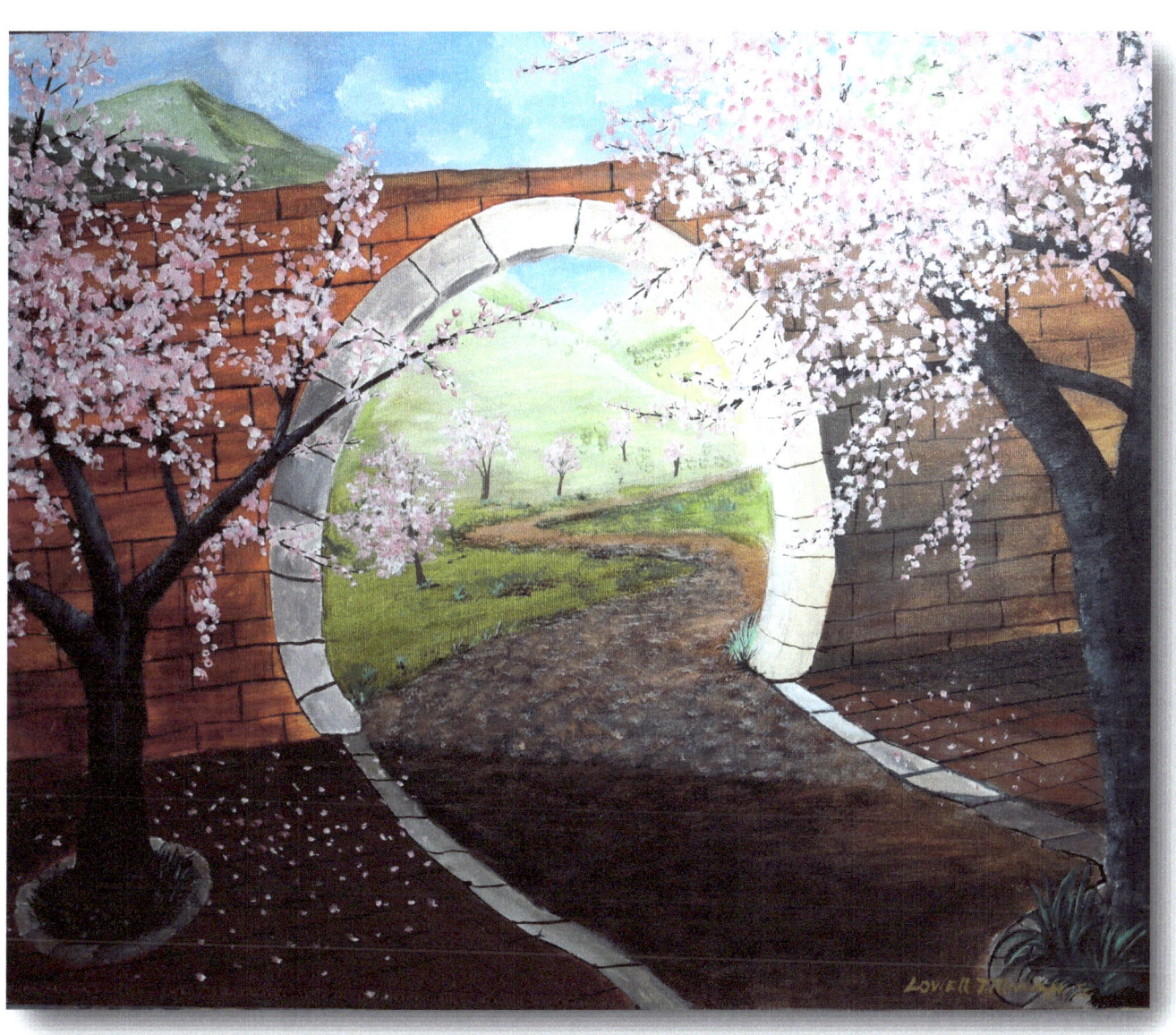

Peaceful Pink

Acrylic 16x20 panel board

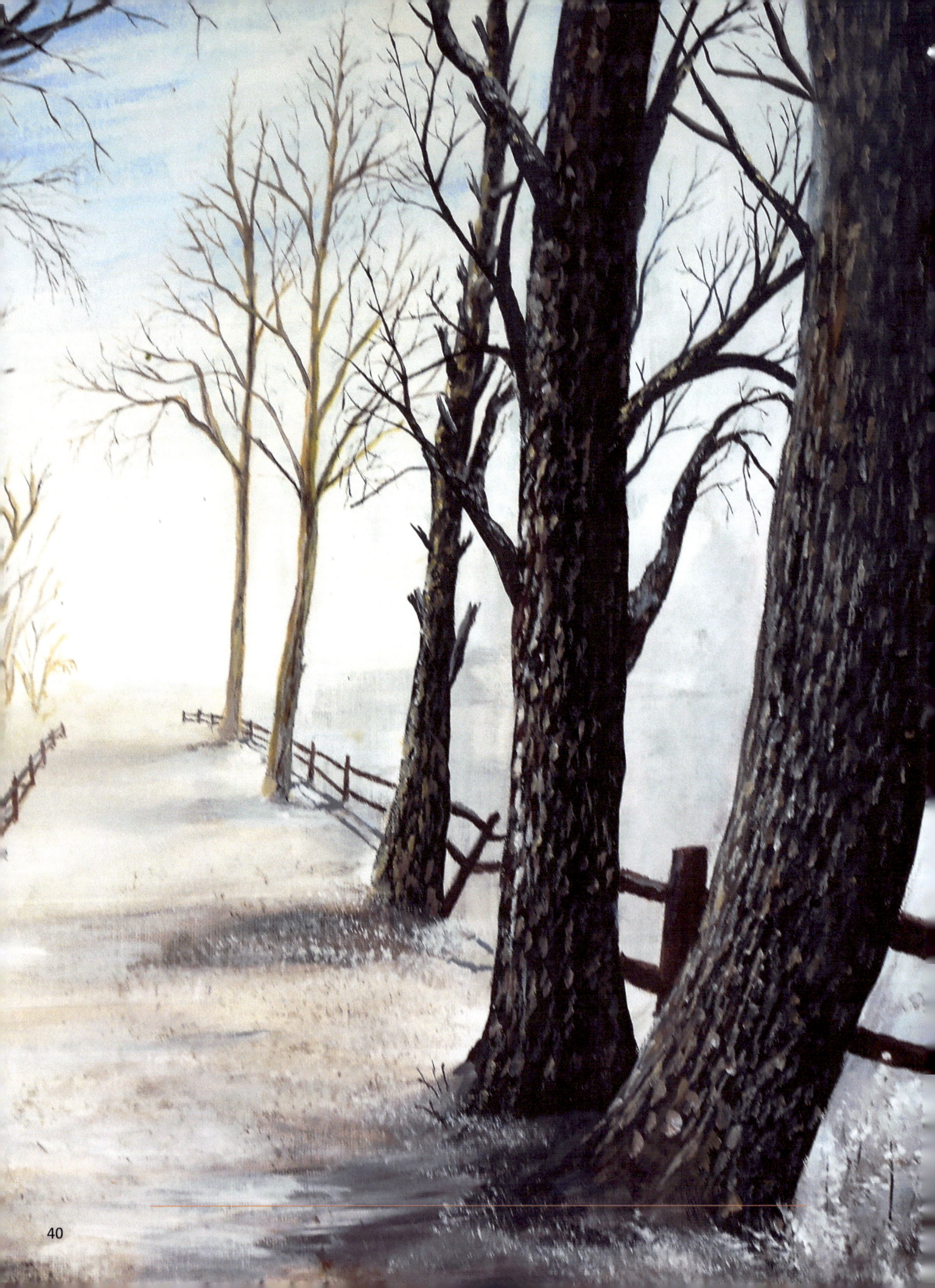

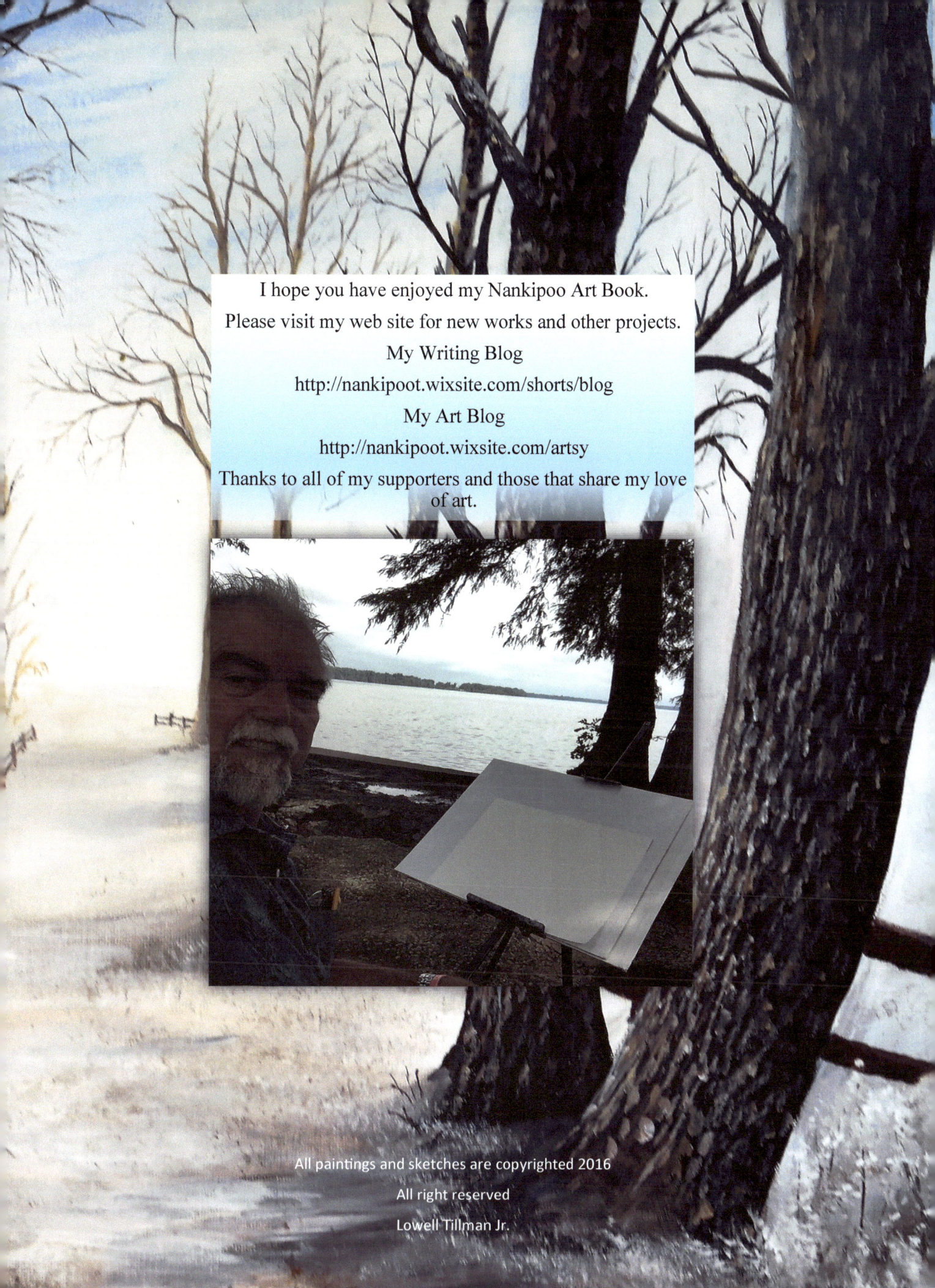

I hope you have enjoyed my Nankipoo Art Book.

Please visit my web site for new works and other projects.

My Writing Blog

http://nankipoot.wixsite.com/shorts/blog

My Art Blog

http://nankipoot.wixsite.com/artsy

Thanks to all of my supporters and those that share my love of art.

All paintings and sketches are copyrighted 2016

All right reserved

Lowell Tillman Jr.

www.ingramcontent.com/pod-product-compliance
Lightning Source LLC
Chambersburg PA
CBHW040441220526
45473CB00004B/1493